Author of *Put Time on Your Side*

JACK SUTHERLAND

TIME TO
CATCH UP

Powerful Strategies to Accelerate
Retirement Funding

TIME TO CATCH UP
Powerful Strategies to Accelerate Retirement Funding

Copyright © 2022   Jack Sutherland

Library of Congress Control Number: 2022938800
                           Paperback: 978-1-958169-32-2
                           eBook: 978-1-958169-33-9

Printed in the United States of America

To

Kora, Jackson, Maya, and Emmanuel.

To all our grandchildren and the next generation facing the challenge of retirement.

CONTENTS

INTRODUCTION

sk one hundred people to describe how they expect to spend their retirement years, and their responses might be that they envision a variety of fun activities, including spending mornings on the golf course; sailing around the world with exotic visits port to port; or afternoons with friends, playing cards, enjoying cocktails, and watching the sunset. To enjoy a retirement anywhere approaching this leisurely lifestyle would require a monthly income of sizable proportions. Unless you have been diligent in saving and investing throughout your career, you can kiss this idyllic picture of retirement goodbye. Instead, plan on working long past your normal retirement age with a lowered expectation of your retirement lifestyle.

Building a nest egg for retirement has never been easy. If it were easy, most of us would have few financial worries as we near full retirement age. That such thinking might exist is a testament to the power of self-delusion. Reality paints a very different picture. Everyone retires eventually, but not everyone is financially prepared for retirement.

Past research has shown more than two-thirds (68 percent) of Americans of working age (twenty-five to sixty-four) did not participate in an employer-sponsored retirement plan. If you do not participate, how can you achieve a positive outcome? The obvious conclusion is too many people are not saving enough for retirement, according to a study in the late 1990s by the Schwartz Center for Economic Policy Analysis.

You say, "Wait a minute; the Social Security tax deducted from my paycheck is more than enough participation in a retirement program." Social security, however, was never intended to replace your preretirement income. It is intended to provide a safety net or threshold level of income for basic living expenses, to be supplemented by other income sources, such as 401(k)s and personal IRAs, investment earnings, and savings. You will not be financially comfortable in a retirement that is solely dependent on Social Security.

The reasons for nonparticipation in plans proliferate like kudzu. Today, more than ever, many people are employed by small businesses that may not offer any type of retirement plan. Likewise, part-time and contract workers may not qualify for company-sponsored plans. Others decline to participate in retirement plans because they are living paycheck to paycheck and need all their earnings to meet current living expenses.

There are hundreds of reasons why people choose not to participate in company retirement plans. They may also ignore investing in other retirement products, like individual retirement accounts (IRAs). Taken together, these are shallow reasons, at best. Anyone with earned income qualifies for a Roth IRA or traditional IRA. Self-directed 401(k) plans are available for those with self-employment income. The motivation to save has to come from within, not from bold statistics that indicate a failure to save will lead to a future retirement of financial hardships. After all, retirement is many years away. Wrong! Do not deceive yourself about how fast the years fly by.

In a more recent study conducted by AARP (American Association of Retired Persons), fifty-five million Americans working full- or part-time private sector jobs lacked access to retirement plan coverage where they worked. The most logical and painless place a person might save for retirement is through an employer-sponsored plan with payroll deductions going automatically into retirement accounts.

According to the *Wall Street Journal*, nearly half of US households did not have a single retirement account in 2013. Among those who did, most had 401(k) plans rather than defined-benefit pension plans.

Participation Rates and Medium Retirement Account Balances

Age Group	Percent That Own Retirement Accounts	Median Retirement Savings
25–34	46.2%	$13,500
35–44	55.4%	$42,700
45–54	56.5%	$87,000
55–64	59.3%	$104,000
All Age Groups 25–64	54.7%	$50,000

Private Sector Workers Only Participating in Employer-Based Retirement Plans

401(k) Only	33%
Defined Benefit Pension Plan Only	2%
Both Plans	11%

SOURCE: National Institute on Retirement Security, 2013

Each of these three cited studies over different periods of time indicates a pending retirement crisis of major underfunded proportions. To avoid being swept up by this tsunami of worry and fear about retirement funding, you are required to take action *now* to accelerate funding for your future retirement.

Without access to such plans, individuals need to break the self-imposed restraints of inertia and initiate their own retirement game plans. Who has the personal responsibility and accountability for providing for you and your family in retirement? After all, the bank of Mom and Dad closed a long time ago. The answer is *you*. The only person preventing you from participating in a plan is also *you*!

About Me

Before I introduce the first chapter, let me share a word about me, the author. I do not sell any financial products. I do not earn fees or commissions for any referrals to financial advisers, insurance agents, or brokers. I earn an income as the managing partner of an alternative investment fund whose focus is lending to small businesses and their owners. I do not believe there is any conflict of interest between what I do for a living and writing this book. There is no overlap between the recommendations I make in this book and how I earn money. What I enjoy doing is writing about and sharing retirement planning strategies based on my personal experience. After forty-plus years as a community banker, I have seen clients with vastly different financial results from a well-planned retirement versus those who never planned. One of the most disappointing and frequently occurring situations is what I call a hybrid retirement plan. This occurs when people start with a retirement plan and good intentions but then become distracted or diverted along the way from fully executing the plan. I use my experience to help you create a plan from scratch or to get back on track in making the funding of your retirement accounts a priority. If I can assist you in achieving a more comfortable retirement and avoid many of the mistakes I have seen others make in my career, then my mission will be accomplished.

About This Book

Maybe it is time to reboot. Our economy is rapidly being reshaped by technology. Employment opportunities are changing throughout the country, driven by the popularity of the Internet and the rise of mobile apps such as Uber and Airbnb. These types of applications have ushered in the era of the sharing economy. Some financial writers have dubbed this the rise of the "gig economy." The idea here is more and more Americans are working as "independent contractors," not full-time employees. Estimates have been as high as one-quarter to one-third of the people in the workforce today no longer hold full-time jobs. They move from gig to gig. These gig workers do not receive benefits through a traditional employer-sponsored plan. This developing trend has negative ramifications for building individual retirement account balances in the future.

Effectively, our economy has entered a mature stage of development where it has a people problem. Not only are we evolving into a gig economy, but we are also witnessing the shrinkage of full-time employees (FTEs) in other ways. Many companies are shifting work traditionally done by FTEs to outsourced contractors. The reason cited has been driven by expense-reduction strategies but this trend threatens overall job security for most employees. Other companies call this the twenty-first-century workforce solution. If this continues, it bodes ill for the number of FTEs needed by industry in the future.

Other studies have shown too many people over the age of fifty still maintain more in debt than in retirement savings. This combination of age, high debt, and low retirement account balances is anathema to most Americans who want a fulfilling retirement experience. These statistics are a reminder of how difficult it is to fully implement transformational financial strategies. We are facing a retirement crisis, just waiting to happen!

Few subjects are more popular, or more confusing, than retirement funding and planning. Preretirees face a number of headwinds: ultra-low interest rates, volatile bond and equity markets, actuarial projections of extended or expected longevity, changing employment opportunities, and a plethora of products and services being sold offering solutions to this retirement conundrum. In the past if your entire career was with one company and that company provided a traditional pension plan upon retirement, these obstacles to achieving a fully funded retirement plan were of less relevance to individuals. The company took care of the funding, and they wrestled with changing market conditions. Today is a different story. Uncertainty is a fact of life!

Corporate-sponsored, fully funded pension plans are becoming extinct! The decline and elimination of traditional pension plans has put the spotlight on the importance of defined contribution plans, like 401(k) s and individual retirement accounts (IRAs). These plans require more individual involvement in decision making, such as the dollar amount to be invested, choosing among investment alternatives, and maintaining the personal financial discipline to continue making contributions until full retirement age.

About the Targeted Audience

Many people do not have the training or desire to take an active role in their retirement plans. Their careers have been built around other areas of expertise, such as teaching, sales, manufacturing, engineering, management, health care, or human resources, to name a few. So how do you achieve a fully funded plan for retirement if you lack a financial background?

This book targets those in midcareer who find themselves below their required level of funding for a secure retirement. I use examples throughout this book of a person age fifty-five, still working, and who has started saving for retirement but has fallen behind on making a contribution amount that will build a sustainable retirement fund. How does this person get back on track and catch up on funding his or her retirement accounts?

If you are a member of the large number of people who have an insufficient level of retirement savings, I am not placing blame on you. The change in how retirement plans are offered to employees has dramatically affected the entire process of saving and investing for retirement. It is not your fault the rules have changed. Your parents may have had careers that provided defined benefit pension plans. For them, saving and investing for retirement was provided by their employer; today, you have to provide for your own retirement. This requires you to take action. What is the appropriate action needed to accomplish your retirement goals?

The answer to this and many other key questions is the subject of this book. I explain the seven strategies of the unique retirement planning model I developed, called "A You-Centered Retirement Model."

A You-Centered Retirement Model

- pay yourself first
- set goals and plan
- pay off debt
- two golden opportunities
- never run out of money
- financial power of attorney
- integrate with Social Security

Contrast this model with either the corporate-centered model or the government-centered model. In both these models, most of the responsibility for funding and providing investment options is with someone else: the corporation or the government agency (municipal, county, state, or federal). Unless you spend your career with one of these two types of employers, you are on your own to provide for your retirement.

About a You-Centered Retirement Model

What is a You-Centered Retirement Model? When is the last time you were the number one priority for anything? Can't remember? That would be the most honest answer. In this model, you are the center of all activities and their resultant outcomes. With this model, you can reboot your retirement-funding priorities. You are *the* priority. The model demonstrates the inter-relationship of seven key strategies working together. When these seven strategies are in full harmony and working smoothly together, you may think of this in terms of a "rising tide lifts all boats" model when it comes to retirement. The details for implementing each of these strategies are explained within the chapters that follow.

What is your role in this model? Your role is that of a conductor or quarterback, meaning you are directing and coordinating each of the components making up your retirement plan with professionals. This model is specific to you. You are asked to make decisions on every aspect of these funding priorities and investment decisions. With this model, you are taking charge of your future!

This model does *not* require you to become a financial expert. Even without formal training in finance, you will be capable of building a successful retirement plan after you implement the strategies of a You-Centered Retirement Model.

Finance can be a maze of bewildering rules, formulas, and terms. By understanding the foundation of finance—the interrelated concepts of time and money—you will be prepared to evaluate numerous individual financial alternatives. Being able to analyze financial alternatives on the basis of risk, return, and appropriateness for your risk tolerance is of vital importance. You already make a similar type of analysis, either tacitly or explicitly, when you decide to spend for consumption rather than save and invest. It is a part of your unconscious decision-making process. I want you to bring this analytic ability to the forefront of your mind and make it a conscious part of every spending decision.

Unless you get started investing now, time will expire before you get focused on retirement. Working longer, having a part-time job, and/or lowering your living expectations in retirement may ultimately be your only choices. Why settle for these dismal consequences?

Time to Catch Up offers clear guidance for those entering their middle years whose retirement plans are behind schedule and need a boost. The strategies outlined in this book are easy to read and understandable. They offer you an opportunity to refresh your thinking about the entire retirement-funding process.

Time is one of the most valuable resources we have. Respect the time you have left before you reach full retirement age, and use it wisely to increase your retirement funding. Do not waste any more time, as now is the time to push retirement funding priorities to the front of your mind. Get your plan across the goal line before the clock runs out. Your retirement years will be more comfortable if you can implement the ideas contained within this book. Success is a conscious decision, and success in retirement planning comes from execution.

About What This Book Cannot Do

Let me be certain you understand what *Time to Catch Up* is not. It will not give you a secret formula to make a quick million dollars or more. I also do not assume you need help with the basics of balancing a checkbook. This book is not for everyone; it was written with a targeted audience in mind that shares some unique circumstances, like an average age of fifty-five or so, and who find themselves stuck in a rut about what to do to ensure their financial self-sufficiency in retirement. Here are a few other common traits of the intended target audience:

- a desire to fund retirement accounts to support a comfortable retirement
- a need to reboot their retirement funding to a higher level
- a willingness to live on less than their income
- the financial discipline to formulate a plan and commit to it
- the will to transform their financial behavior now for a future benefit

Throughout this book, I place a tremendous emphasis on *your* plans, *your* goals, and *your* financial well-being. In my experience, one of the most dangerous actions you can take is to delegate your personal financial planning completely to a financial adviser, a CPA, an attorney, or any other trusted adviser. Your goals, aspirations, and dreams are what form the foundation of *your* plan, not someone else's or a canned financial model. Simply filling in the blanks will not make it your plan.

Webster's Dictionary defines retirement as "the action or fact of leaving one's job and ceasing to work." To me this is an old-school definition. This can be a frightening time for a lot of people, but it doesn't have to be. What do you want retirement to mean for you? You can write your own definition.

If you are unhappy maintaining the status quo of your current retirement funding, then this book has been written for *you*. If you have been trapped by inaction because of worries about family, career, and aging parents, what are you waiting for? Inertia remains the primary force in delaying or avoiding retirement planning. Take ownership of your retirement planning and funding and move into action by reading this book. Let's get started!

PART 1

PREPARATION

Chapter 1

....

The Relationship between Time and Money

T he road leading to achieving financial freedom in retirement is full of curves and potholes, but it all starts with you. As stated, this book will provide guidance for people entering their middle years who need to increase funding for their retirement. The book will bring you back on course from any detour you may have taken. By definition, this age bracket places you in a demographic group known as late-stage baby boomers or generation X, with birth years up to 1981. For the purposes of this book, I assume you are fifty-five years old today, and I will use this same age in most of the examples cited. For this age group, full retirement age is sixty-seven (the age you qualify for full Social Security benefits) or only twelve years away. The book also assumes you are employed and have had some time to begin saving and funding a retirement account through either plans at work or using other forms of saving and retirement accounts, such as individual retirement accounts or self-directed 401(k) plans.

Money issues have been known to cause individuals both stress and joy. For example, people frequently worry about

- not having enough money for their everyday expenses;
- not earning enough to save anything on a regular basis; and
- not having enough funds later in life to provide financial assistance for their aging parents, siblings, or other loved ones.

In addition, they often have concerns about

- how to distribute money evenly in an estate plan;
- how to provide for a college education for their kids or grandchildren;
- how to avoid making bad decisions that could drain their nest egg; and
- how to avoid outliving their retirement nest egg.

It seems like the stress factors outweigh the joy factors for most people. The issues seem to be ubiquitous in your life. Somehow, your personal retirement funding priority gets lost in this jumble of overriding, everyday concerns about money. These fears and worries need to be brought under control and put to rest. I know it is easier said than done, but this is how you start. Be confident that you can achieve financial freedom in retirement. Many others have. Why not you?

One of the secrets to accumulating retirement funds is putting compound interest to work. Invested money earning a return can multiply faster using this proven approach. Money earning more money is another way to think about this mathematical wonder. You may prefer to think of compound interest as the difference between cash contributed to investments today and the actual future value of that investment. With compounding, the increased growth potential of an investment as earnings are reinvested, and the value of your assets accelerate over time.

The essential requirement in making compound interest work in your favor is time. Unless there is enough time to let interest accrue on previously earned interest, the magic of this formula will not work as well as intended. Start investing early, and stay with your plan. If you have not started, you must start now! You have twelve years in this example to make compound interest work for you.

The growth power of compound interest on long-term assets like retirement plans is one of the most effective uses of this concept. Combining the longer time horizon with the deferred-tax status of most retirement plans gives these plans a potential supercharged growth trajectory. Always maximize the use of tax-deferred investing for retirement funding. More on this topic in chapter 8.

Here is a basic example of compound interest working for you:

- Assume you start saving $5,000 per year at age fifty-five earning 7.0 percent interest for fifteen years in a tax-deferred account. The future value of this investment will be $125,655. Your cash in totals $75,000.
- Assume you invest $5,000 per year beginning at age thirty-five earning 7.0 percent interest for thirty-five years in a tax-deferred account. The future value of this investment is $472,405. Your total cash in totals $154,508.
- Which retirement balance would you prefer? The account balance with $346,750 more is the obvious choice.

This example illustrates the power of compound interest and the influence of time on its ability to grow investments. This is the basic foundation of all finance: the interrelationship between time and money.

Here are three more examples of compound interest relating to more realistic contributions to a retirement account. While the beginning dollar amount of retirement savings is different in each example, the other variables are the same. The identical variables are: your current age is fifty-five; twelve years remain for full retirement benefits (age sixty-seven); investments are held in tax-deferred accounts like IRA and 401(k) plans; the annual growth rate is 7.0 percent (below the historical growth rate of the equity market of 9.0 percent+); regular monthly contributions are made throughout the full twelve years; fees are not taken into consideration. The goal of each example is to accumulate a minimum of $500,000 in retirement funds by age sixty-seven. What will be the required monthly/annual amount to be invested to achieve this goal in each scenario?

- Scenario #1: Assume you start with *zero* savings for retirement. *$2,500/month or $30,000 annually = $574,219*

- Scenario #2: Assume you start with $50,000 in various retirement accounts.
  $1,000/month or $12,000 annually = $565,014
- Scenario #3: Assume you have $100,000 in retirement funds in the beginning.
  $500/month or $6,000 annually = $451,421

Again, these examples clearly illustrate the power of compound interest working for you over the full twelve-year period. It is an obvious advantage to start with some dollar amount of retirement savings. This allows the monthly contributions to be smaller and more manageable. If you are participating in a company-sponsored 401(k) plan and receive a company match for your contributions, these monthly numbers will be even lower. There will be more information on the importance of a 401(k) company match in chapter 8. Other strategies to reduce these monthly contribution amounts are outlined in chapter 8 as well.

The relationship between time and money is a symbiotic one. One assists the other in accelerating the growth of your individual contributions. Neither is effective without the other. Combine these two factors with the tax-deferred status of retirement accounts and you have an unbeatable solution to achieving a fully funded retirement.

It is critical that you understand this relationship between time and money if you are to achieve financial freedom. There can be no more excuses for delaying the implementation of a funding strategy for retirement.

It may be hard to imagine, but putting a little extra money into your retirement account weekly can make a big difference in the total accumulated over time. Where can you find more money for savings? Make just a few small changes in your daily routine and you will uncover some extra dollars for retirement. Buying fast food, using vending machines and bringing home take out dinners can add up. If you spend $5 each weekday for food on the go, that becomes $108 a month or

$1,300 a year. This is food you could have just as easily made at home for less money. If you purchase bottled water just three times a week, at $2 a bottle you are spending $6 a week, $26 a month and $312 a year for something that flows freely from the faucet. Why not refill your own water bottle? These ideas may not seem like much but they add up. If you put these same dollars into your retirement account, you will have a larger retirement balance when you retire.

Today is the day to develop a *sense of urgency* about your future. You are the responsible person, no one else.

Foundation of Finance
Time – Money – Compound Interest
All Interrelated and Working Together for You

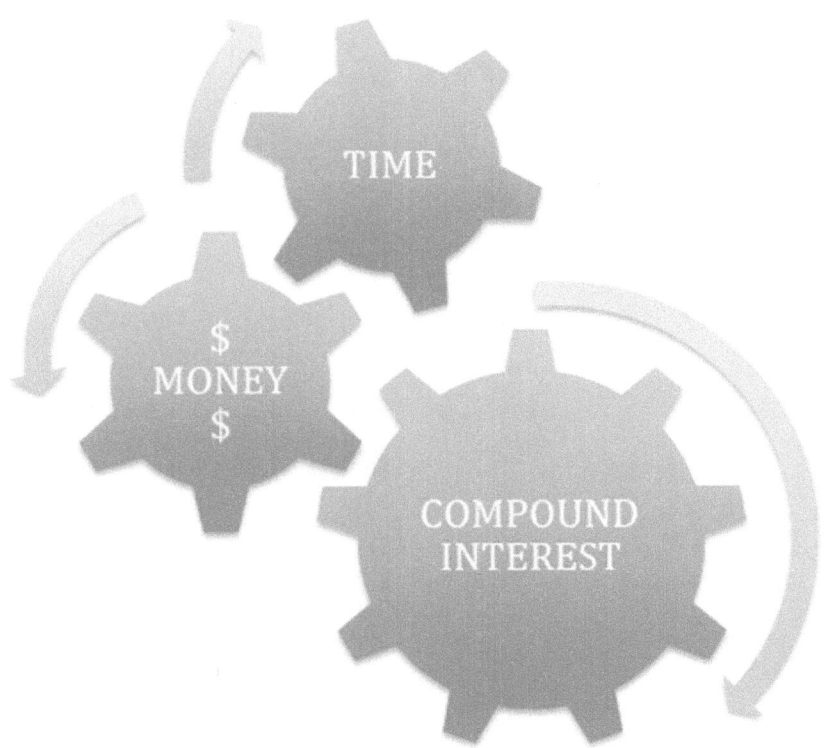

Chapter 2

....

Pay Yourself First

"Pay yourself first" is the first of the seven most important concepts in funding your retirement accounts. It is the fundamental base upon which your financial goals can begin to be realized. You hear this phrase often in retirement literature, but what does "pay yourself first" really mean? Why do so many people ignore this common-sense advice? How much should you pay yourself? How do you get started implementing this concept?

Let's start with a look at how most people manage their salary. The most common payroll period is payment every two weeks. Some people receive a paycheck in their hands while others have their paycheck automatically deposited into their bank account by their employer. Under both payment methods, the amount received is after all taxes have been withheld. What you receive is called the after-tax amount or net pay.

Taxes vary from state to state, but they always include deductions for federal tax, state tax, and Social Security tax, and sometimes local taxes. Federal tax rates are different for each employee based on total adjusted gross income. Let's assume a federal tax rate of 28 percent, a state tax rate of 6 percent, plus Social Security tax withholding and unemployment taxes. Added together, it is not uncommon for theses tax deductions to total 35 to 40 percent of every dollar earned. What does this tell you? Government at the federal, state, and local levels is getting paid first!

Your net pay represents only 60 to 65 percent of what you have earned. This amount is what is left for living expenses, investing, and discretionary spending. From net pay most people then allocate payments among their various bills, to buy food, medicines, and other health care services, for transportation, and maybe for some discretionary spending like eating out, going to the movies, or even a new pair of shoes. Where is the money to come from for investing for retirement?

This example illustrates the difficult position people contend with each month with allocating their net pay. Assume you make a salary of $45,000 annually. This is your gross salary. With the various tax deductions totaling 35 percent of gross salary, you are really earning $29,250 (or 65 percent of the gross salary number). This is your net pay. This is what you have to live on. If taxes increase over time, your net pay will decrease, unless you receive a pay raise. Is it any wonder so many people feel the squeeze between paying for living expenses versus setting money aside for retirement?

Now if I told you there was a way to have access to your hard-earned salary dollars *before* all the tax deductions, would you be interested? This alternative has been available since 1974 with the passage of the Pension Reform Act. This act provided for tax-qualified pension plans, such as corporate pension plans, profit-sharing plans, a Keogh plan, or an individual retirement account (IRA), to be deemed tax-deferred accounts. Yet a large percentage of consumers have failed to pay attention to this potential life-changing opportunity. It is a financial opportunity you should begin to use today. Yes, it is a perfectly legal way to get in front of the tax-withholding government entities.

The majority of Americans do not pay themselves first. The government has stepped to the front of the line on payday by deducting taxes before you receive your net pay. The only way to pay yourself first is by using a *pretax retirement account.* Whether you work for a corporate or noncorporate employer, the Economic Recovery Tax Act of 1981 allows you to contribute to an individual retirement account (IRA), even if you already participate in an employer-sponsored pension or profit-sharing plan. Further, if your spouse is not employed, you can make an additional contribution for the benefit of the spouse. Both types of contributions are subject to limitations, which will be discussed later.

Now you know what it means to pay yourself first. Pay yourself before taxes are withheld from your gross salary. Why do so many Americans ignore this common-sense advice? You saw earlier in the introduction the large percentage of working Americans who do not participate in any employer-sponsored retirement plans. This group also has ignored other options available for accumulating retirement savings. The reasons given have been discussed. What it boils down to is this: Many individuals are not focused on retirement planning. They are overwhelmed with meeting the daily living expenses of their families. They refuse to take responsibility for their retirement and do not want to be held accountable for their lack of planning. Retirement seems so far away. They will worry about retirement plans later. Their priority is living in the moment; the future will be kicked down the road like the proverbial kick-the-can game. This is why we have a looming retirement crisis!

If you want to pay yourself first, how much should you pay yourself? Seems like a fair question. Remember that retirement funding is only one of the demands on your salary, so the amount to pay yourself needs to take into consideration other financial obligations. The amount you pay yourself will need to be a meaningful number if you want to achieve financial freedom in retirement. Most financial advisers recommend saving 10 to 15 percent of your gross pay to be applied toward retirement. In the example of the person earning $45,000 gross pay annually, a savings of $6,750 each year is the target (45,000 x 15% = 6,750). If you look at this number as a monthly contribution, the monthly number is $562.50 or $18.75 daily. This seems a more manageable number. If you cannot start with paying yourself first at this 15 percent rate, reduce the amount initially and increase payments gradually until you reach this 15 percent savings goal.

We have answered the questions: What does pay yourself first mean? Why do people ignore this advice? How much should I pay myself annually or monthly? Now how do you get started? Signing up to participate in a company-sponsored retirement plan is the first step. If you have access to a company-sponsored 401(k) plan, sign up to contribute an amount equivalent to any company match, at a minimum. If your employer will match 3 percent of your annual salary, subject only to you contributing an equal amount, then you should contribute at least 3.0 percent. A 3.0 percent contribution would be $1,350 annually or $112.50 per month ($45,000 x 3.0%). At the end of the year, your employer would contribute $1,350 to your retirement account as well (matching 3 percent). This employer match usually has a vesting schedule, meaning only a portion of the company match becomes yours to keep over a stated time (the vesting schedule). A typical vesting schedule might be five years; this means that 20 percent of the company match becomes yours to keep each year of the first five years of participation. After five years, the entire company match is yours (fully vested). Vesting schedules have been called golden handcuffs, or a way to reduce employee turnover and keep you on the payroll for at least five years to earn the full corporate match.

If you work for an employer that does not offer any retirement alternatives, you can still open an IRA, either a Roth or traditional IRA. If you are self-employed, you can open a self-directed 401(k) plan. The point is this: *open a pretax retirement account,* and fund it with up to 15 percent of your gross income annually, subject to a few limitations. If you already participate in a company-sponsored retirement plan or have an IRA account, all you need to do is increase your contribution to pay yourself at least 15 percent of your gross pay.

This first step was easy. The next step is even easier! To eliminate any chance you may forget to write a check to pay yourself first going forward, put the retirement contribution amount on autopilot. Sign up for a payroll deduction where you work or establish an automatic bank transfer to your retirement trustee to fund your account every month.

That is all there is to it. You are now on your way to achieving financial freedom in retirement.

I know there still may be some skeptics out there, saying it just cannot be that easy. This group of naysayers may need more convincing by understanding the potential cost to them *if they do not pay themselves first.* Remember the employee making $45,000 a year? If that person wanted to invest 15 percent (45,000 x 15% = 6,750) annually (or 562.50 monthly or 18.75 daily) in a tax-deferred retirement account for the next twelve years, earning 7 percent, how much would this sum become by the end of twelve years? That number approximates to $129,000. This is what it will cost you if you do not follow these simple steps. That's a lot of money to leave on the table. H. L. Mencken observed, "The chief value of money lies in the fact that one lives in a world where it is over estimated." He said this more than sixty years ago. I imagine it is more relevant today in our economy fixated on all money matters. Don't leave $129,000 on the table! This amount could represent more than 25 percent of a fully funded retirement account.

Chapter 3

Do You Know Your Personal Net Worth?

I was a community banker for more than forty years. It always astounded me over that span of time how many individuals had no idea about the value of their personal or family net worth. Maybe it was the financial term *net worth* or another intimidating factor that was holding them back. When asked about their net worth, their eyes glazed over or they developed that deer-in-the-headlights look. Knowing your personal or family net worth is not about bragging rights, nor is it intended to impose a sense of guilt for whatever the net worth number. Knowing your net worth is all about measuring progress from where you currently stand in your financial life. The purpose of calculating net worth is to establish a baseline to evaluate where you are financially and to give you access to a proper measurement tool for comparing your progress year after year.

We perform a similar measurement process with our grading system for students. The academic progress of the student is reflected by grades on report cards. The same is true with medical checkups. Once a patient has had an annual physical to establish a baseline for blood pressure and other bodily functions, future visits to the doctor's office are measured against the previous baseline for any changes, good or bad. It's the same with automotive checkups. The mileage, tire, and brake wear and operations under the hood are evaluated for the need for additional service or replacement. Why would we not perform a similar measure for financial progress in our personal lives?

What is net worth? The simple definition of net worth is assets minus liabilities. It is a point-in-time view of the dollar amount of financial reserves available to fund future needs, such as retirement. Net worth is *not* income, which many people believe is the only important measuring tool for financial well-being. Net worth can be calculated for an individual, a family, or a business entity. The most common form of net worth calculation is using a joint financial statement (joint for husband and wife). If you prepare an individual financial statement, care should be taken to only include assets in your personal name and divide ownership in any assets held in joint name. It is very difficult to determine the exact ownership percentage of joint assets held within a family. For our purposes, let us work with an example calculating net worth using a joint financial statement.

A sample joint financial statement form is shown at exhibit 1. Take a few minutes to familiarize yourself with this form and the basic information required for completion. These are similar forms used by your banker or other lenders when you request a loan or when you are asked to provide updated information for the bankers' files. Accuracy is paramount. Financial statement fraud can result when people try to scam the system by falsifying a financial statement. This is a serious breach of the law and subject to prosecution.

The form seems self-explanatory. In the interest of clarification, here are a few definitions to guide you in the preparation of a joint financial statement. Date the financial statement as of the date of the information used to complete the form. Year-end or month-end dates are the most commonly used. Assets are the things you and your spouse *own*. They are listed at the top of the form. Assets can have different values based on cost, current market value, or a future multiple of market value based on some anticipated action that will add value over time. The most conservative value is the cost method when used for real estate and personal assets. Financial investments should be shown at current market value as of the date of the financial statement. Ownership of any privately owned business should be shown as the net worth on the most recent financial statement for that business. Cash value of life insurance is *not* face value or death benefit of the policies. Cash value is a stated value within the policy that you can access as a loan, if needed.

Liabilities are what you and your spouse *owe*. Most liabilities have monthly statements provided by the lender detailing the current balance of what is owed. Use the most current monthly statement as of the date of your financial statement for each liability.

Net worth is the result of subtracting total liabilities from total assets. This is the number to use in tracking your progress toward achieving financial freedom in retirement. Take some time now to fill in the information for your joint financial statement. The resulting net worth number will give you a starting point to measure your progress toward achieving your financial goals. I recommend copying the exhibit to allow you to have several blank copies to work with as you compute your personal, joint net worth.

Completing a joint financial statement gives you an opportunity to review it with your spouse. I recommend this exercise on an annual basis. For me, the best time to complete the joint financial statement is around tax-filing season. By then I have all my year-end statements available, and it is relatively easy to complete the form. The financial statement would be dated as of the end of the year. If the resulting net worth number does not show the type of financial progress you were expecting, the discussion with your spouse will take a different path and could include ideas to make adjustments needed to get back on track. Reducing expenses, increasing retirement funding, paying down debt, and living within your means are a few of the topics that might be on the agenda. Calculating your joint net worth annually is an important process, not just a paperwork exercise. Put it in the same category as annual tax filing. It is a tool that will help you measure your progress toward achieving a longer-term plan, like retirement funding.

Chapter 4

....

The Role of Budgeting

This is not going to be a tutorial on budgeting. At this stage of life (age fifty-five), you already know the importance of budgeting to match expenses with your income. Life has already taught you that expenses must be managed to be able to live the lifestyle you currently enjoy. So why are so many people entering the last chapters of their working life without adequate savings and a debt burden weighing them down?

I am not naïve in assuming budgeting is easy. Budgeting is a chore! Making a budget and sticking with it is one of the two most difficult things I think we do. The other is following a diet. I have struggled with one and failed at the other, so I enter the discussion about the role of budgeting with some trepidation. Both budgeting and dieting require a strong dose of self-discipline, if they are to be helpful tools in reaching your goals. Most of us have self-discipline until the moment we are tempted to do something different with our money or consume foods not included on a diet. Then it all breaks down, and we give up on the budget or diet and just "wing it" as we move forward in life. My personal experience has proven it is all right to veer off these restrictive parameters of budgeting money once in a while. My experience with breaking a diet is not as good. We are human, after all. After falling off the wagon, the key is getting back on budget as soon as you can. I want you to commit to maintaining self-discipline with your budget, no matter what. Once you make budgeting part of your normal practice, it becomes a habit.

At that point, budgeting becomes more automatic every time you think about spending money.

Maybe it is time to take a fresh look at the role of budgeting. Let's start with the goal of budgeting. It is not to track every dollar spent; it is to help us control spending and focus our spending on what really matters. The goal of budgeting is to change our financial behavior. This is no small task. Simply stated, to generate adequate investments for retirement, living on less than you make is a must. It is no more complicated than that. Budgeting should be your compass to keep you on the road to financial freedom, not a dull exercise of recording income and expense numbers and then filing them away in a drawer. Budgeting should provide answers to how and where you spend money, what is the gap between income and expenses, how much is available for investment, and how many dollars for discretionary spending can you manage each month. If your current budgeting process does not answer all four of these questions, then you should put yourself through a refresher budgeting course.

Active budgeting is a dynamic process. This means the numbers change from month to month to reflect the reality of your lifestyle. Start with a monthly look at your expenses. After you have recorded your actual monthly expenses, analyze whether you are over or under your monthly income. If you are digging a financial hole, something has to change. Make a conscious decision to reduce expenses where you can. After recording the second month of actual expenses, follow the same routine until you finally have the monies to fund your retirement accounts. After about a year of doing this monthly exercise, you are now prepared to construct a budget for the coming year. Project next year's expenses on the basis of the revised monthly budgets from the previous year. Going forward in year two, you can compare your actual expenses against this annual budget. Remember to divide the annual budget categories by twelve to compare expenses on a monthly basis. Variances, good and bad, should be explained. Active budgeting will require you to take action any month to adjust components of your budget that are not in agreement with the original budget. Is the budget variance an outlier, a result from faulty budgeting, or an indication of a permanent increase in certain expense categories? You may be able to explain short-term variances that will come back into alignment next month. Examples might be unplanned automotive expenses, sudden illness requiring higher medical bills, or a roof repair caused by a storm. The point is you will need to take action to realign spending with income when this variance occurs.

In chapter 2 the concept of "pay yourself first" was discussed. Nowhere is this more important than its implementation in the budgeting process. If you budget to make a $562.50 monthly contribution to your retirement account, that becomes a priority. Make that contribution first each month to avoid running out of money before you fund your retirement.

Another role of budgeting is to highlight where you are spending money. The only way to reduce expenses is to first understand where your money goes. All of us can find a way to reduce our monthly expenses, if we are dedicated to funding our retirement goals. Here are a few examples of easy ways to personally save money:

- Reduce dining at fast food establishments or restaurants rather than eating at home.
- Eliminate wearing clothing requiring dry cleaning rather than wash and wear.
- Control impulse purchases like buying a pair of shoes we do not need.
- Substitute buying Starbucks coffee with buying cheaper brands like McDonald's.
- Eliminate a landline at home that is not being used.
- Downsize to a smaller house or apartment.
- Drive the car one more year rather than trading for a newer model.

These examples are only the tip of the iceberg, if you are really serious about finding ways to reduce expenses. You should develop your own list. By starting to save now, you are taking advantage of the interrelationship between time and money by letting compound interest go to work. Here are my ten easiest ways to reduce common household expenses:

1. Enroll in a 401(k) plan and reduce your taxes.
2. Adjust tax-withholding on your salary; if you always get a tax refund, adjust your withholding number lower and bank the difference.
3. Increase auto insurance deductibles, which will result in lower premiums.
4. Pay off all credit card debt; this is a no brainer.
5. Use public transportation where possible; you will save on parking, tolls and auto maintenance.
6. Brown-bag your lunch; save the high cost of eating out.
7. Reshop your auto insurance annually, looking for the best deal.
8. Eat at home more often; cooking saves money.
9. Change cell phone plans by shopping around for the best deal.
10. If you use credit cards, use one that offers rewards of cash back and/or airplane miles.

Expense reduction should be the focus of your efforts because we have more control over expenses. Most of us do not have jobs that provide a variable income. We have a fixed salary. Commission salespeople would be one example of a variable income stream. Another example is someone working strictly on an hourly basis. The more hours worked, the more income.

The point of reducing expenses is to find additional funds for investing for retirement. Yes, there may be some pain in some of these decisions, but a lifestyle in retirement with financial freedom will be more appealing than if you refuse to make these choices now. Make active budgeting a part of your regular routine. It will help guide you down the path to a more worry-free retirement. It is up to you. See exhibit 3 for an annual budgeting format that has proven to be helpful in identifying spending trends. Careful analysis of these trends will show you what you can change today to increase savings for tomorrow.

"Too much of a good thing," said Mae West, "can be wonderful." This does not apply to budgeting. Do not be a slave to your budget. Flexibility and adjustments over time will be essential in making a dynamic budget work for you. No one else has your exact set of circumstances to deal with on a daily basis. They may be similar but not exactly the same. Life is for living, and you are the only one who can guide your saving activities toward a goal of financial freedom in retirement.

There are many examples of budgeting spreadsheets and ideas online. Several websites worthy of consideration include the following:

- www.quicken.com
- www.mint.com
- www.budgettracker.com

See exhibit 2 for a very basic paper copy of a monthly budget format for recording expenses.

Budgeting is a tool. It is not the end all of financial planning. Use it to help you understand that you are in charge of your financial condition. You have full authority to decide how and where you spend money. A budget can help you change your financial behavior. A budget should ultimately grant you freedom from financial worry, not drown you in boredom. Make it work for you!

Chapter 5

....

Goal Setting: Develop a Plan

H ow do you achieve a goal if you do not have one? Think of a goal as a target. If you were on the shooting range, the target allows you to instantly know the location of the target, the direction to shoot, the approximate distance to target, and make any adjustments needed for wind, sun glare and terrain, and it shows you the size of the bull's-eye. With this knowledge, your chances of hitting the target are exponentially better than if the shooting range had no targets. Sound ridiculous?

Think of goals another way. What if you boarded an airplane and on your way into the cabin you asked the pilot what time you would be arriving at your destination? If the pilot said, "I don't know because flight control has not told me where we are flying today," how would you feel about your flight? I'm guessing you would be very nervous and maybe ask to deplane as soon as possible. After all, it is impossible to arrive at a destination if you do not know where you are going!

This is a similar scenario shared by many Americans who go to work every day and put in their time waiting for retirement. They have no destination (goals), live paycheck-to-paycheck, and refuse to plan for their future, including retirement. Somehow they hope there will be money available for their retirement from some unknown source. This is not a plan; it is a dream headed toward a nightmare!

Goals should be written to help keep us on track. Written goals also keep us from changing them every time some obstacle gets in the way of achieving them. People have a way of forgetting, modifying, and abandoning goals when times are tough. Truly committed goal achievers do not let any obstacle divert them from their mission.

Goals can be short or long term. Goals for retirement need to be long term and very specific. In our example of a person of age fifty-five who wants to retire by age sixty-seven, what would be a sensible financial goal? To say I want to be rich in retirement is not a goal. I want enough in retirement to live comfortably is not a goal. These are nothing more than hopes and wishes for a better future. If you decide you need to accumulate $500,000 in your retirement accounts by age sixty-seven, that is a goal, and it is both specific and long term (twelve years). This is a reasonable retirement goal at your current age. Where did I get this goal of $500,000? Fidelity Investments estimates that to retire comfortably, a person should accumulate at least ten times his or her final annual salary (previous example of $45,000 x 10 = $450,000 rounded up to $500,000).

If you are the type of person who jumps ahead and reads the last chapter of a novel first because you want to know the ending before you start the book, you may be asking, "Just tell me the retirement number I need to save to live a comfortable retirement. Forget all the preparation, execution, and other analytics in planning. Just give me the number!" There is no easy answer. Every individual has so many variables that to give you an answer is to run the risk of oversimplification. Beyond all the preliminary work, actuary tables, and future value calculations, the simplistic answer may be found using one of the many online retirement calculators. While the single number given by most of these calculators may be suspect, because we do not know all of the assumptions built into the various algorithms driving these calculators, that number can be an indicator of your future goal. For most people, this may be all they are looking for. See exhibit 4 for a sample worksheet to assist you in determining your retirement number. If you do not like worksheets, below is a list of online calculators I have found useful, each providing an indication *only* of a potential, future retirement savings goal. These interactive calculators are intended to be used as self-help tools. They cannot be guaranteed to be totally applicable or accurate in regard to your individual circumstances. All calculators are hypothetical models, so be cautious when using them:

- Vanguard Retirement Income Calculator
- apps.finra.org
- www.bankrate.com
- www.schwab.com
- www.aarp.org

Planning is the second strategy of a You-Centered Retirement Model. Now that you have committed this goal to writing, the next step is to develop a plan to achieve the goal. There are two parts in retirement plan development: those requiring immediate action and others needing long-term nurturing. The first step is to fund a reserve account to cover living expenses for your family for up to six months. Look at your budget to determine how much your living expenses have been for the past six months. Add these monthly expense totals together to see how much you need in a cash reserve account. I call this a rainy day fund or an amount of money needed to cover any unexpected expenses or basic living expenses if you were fired, were laid off, or could not work for any reason. This emergency cash should be kept in a very liquid form, like a bank account or money market account with a mutual fund. To fund this account, establish a monthly deposit directly into the account. If you can, automate the monthly deposit. This ensures you never forget to write a check. I recommend you start with 10 to 15 percent of your gross salary, and remember to pay yourself first. Here are the numbers for this example requiring immediate action:

$$\$45,000 \times 15\% = \$6,750 \text{ annual contribution}$$
$$\text{or } \$562.50 \text{ monthly or } \$18.75 \text{ daily}$$

I recommend dividing these numbers by two and use half the amount to fund the cash reserve account and the other half to flow into retirement accounts. This way you are feeding two goals at the same time. Keep adding to this cash reserve account until the total equates to your basic living expenses for a six-month period. When you achieve an appropriate cash reserve account balance, you can direct 100 percent of your contribution to funding your retirement accounts.

The second phase of this immediate activity in funding your retirement plan is to decide where to deposit the funds and in what type of account. If you already have a 401(k) account, adding to this account is a no brainer. The same is true if you already have an individual retirement account (IRA). If you do not have either account, then it is time to open one or both for your monthly contributions.

There are many alternative trustees available for a self-directed IRA or Roth IRA. These include American Century Investments, Charles Schwab, the Vanguard Group, or Fidelity Investments, to mention a few. Research online information about the requirements, minimum investment amount, fees, and any restrictions applicable for each vendor. Select a vendor you can be comfortable with, and then choose the types of investments you want in your account. Here I recommend the KISS principle: keep it simple and sustainable. This concludes the activity requiring immediate action. Now you can focus on the longer-term needs of retirement funding.

General rules of thumb are just that. They are very general, but they can be useful. Be cautious in using them, as they may not apply to your specific circumstances. Beware of blindly following rules of thumb quoted in the news or by financial advisers. Making investment decisions for your retirement accounts is your opportunity to tailor-make a plan you can live with over time.

The basics of any retirement investment plan should include some mix of equities (stocks), bonds, and cash. This process is called asset allocation. The exact dollar amount or percentage of total investment allocated to each category is up to you.

Now I know many people get nervous when it comes to talking about the equity market. Your grandparents or great-grandparents may have lived through the Great Depression, and their stories of financial hardship have become legend in family gatherings. Do not let this fear of the unknown keep you from taking the risk to achieve a potential higher return on your invested dollars. Daily headlines and lead stories on the evening news carry each day's stock market performance, whether the market was up or down. On the days when the market losses are high, you may be breathing a sigh of relief that you are not in the market. This is a mistake. While it may sound counterintuitive, you need to be in the market all the time with your retirement accounts. This is called staying fully invested. Stocks and mutual funds offer the best potential for growth. You should not be focused on daily market changes. Keep your eye on the longer-term objectives. I am recommending only a portion of your funds be invested in equities.

Any daily fluctuation in the value of stocks creates what is called unrealized gains or losses. Unless you sell specific stocks on that particular day, you have not experienced a real gain or loss. Your retirement accounts are long term in nature, and today's value is not as important as the future value of those accounts at full retirement age. Maybe for your peace of mind, you might consider looking at the value of your retirement accounts monthly or quarterly, rather than daily.

I want to take a short time-out at this point to clarify what type of investments I am suggesting. When I talk about stocks, equities, bonds, fixed income, mutual funds, and other investment options, I am always referring to passively managed index funds. These also include exchange traded funds (ETF), as well. Actively managed funds have higher fees, and their managers are trying to *outperform* the market. Passively managed funds have lower fees and their managers are trying to *match* the market. There is a big difference in the historical performance of these two types of managers. Passively managed index funds have outperformed their counterparts consistently over the past ten years.

Passive funds have less frequent trading and several other factors that help reduce both fees and taxes. Taxes were reduced an average of 0.96 percent point a year off the returns of some two thousand actively managed US stock funds over a fifteen-year period that ended in September 2014, if they were held in taxable accounts rather than tax-sheltered retirement accounts. This finding was according to research by Vanguard Group. By contrast, taxes reduced the returns of 130 broad-based US stock index funds by an average of 0.69 percent a year over the same period. A lower tax impact is better and demonstrates a greater tax efficiency. So there is a win-win with index funds/ETFs: lower fees and lower taxes than actively managed funds.

What is an ETF? Created in 1993, an exchange traded fund (ETF) is a marketable security that tracks an index like an index fund. Unlike mutual funds, an ETF trades like a common stock but offers diversification. They have price changes throughout the day while mutual fund shares are priced at the end of each trading day with the net asset value (NAV) of the fund. Typically, fees are lower with an ETF than a mutual fund and may enjoy some tax advantages. One of the most widely known ETFs tracks the S&P 500 and is called SPIDER (SPY). Another is the QQQ, which tracks the Nasdaq 100, and the DIA tracks the Dow Jones Industrial average. Today there are more than eighteen hundred ETF funds valued at more than $2.7 trillion, according to research firm XTF.

After extensive research, it seems to me that an appropriate mix of equities and bonds to provide for the potential of growth, inflation protection, and diversification while achieving an acceptable risk-adjusted rate of return is the place to start. For our reader at age fifty-five, possibly with a family still at home, such a model portfolio allocation might look like this, depending on your investment style. You choose the style best suited to your investing approach:

Investment	Conservative	Balanced	Growth	Aggressive
Equities	70%	50%	80%	90%
Bonds	25%	50%	15%	10%
Cash	5%	Zero	5%	Zero

Conservative, Balanced, Growth, Aggressive

The table above is ordered from least (conservative) to most risk (aggressive).

You can tweak these percentages in either direction, depending on your personal preference. Within each of these investment styles, equities should include a mix of small-company, midsize, and large-company stocks to achieve diversification. Perhaps a plan with this mix of stocks would be a comfortable allocation for you within the equity portion of your portfolio:

- small-company stock index 15 percent
- midsize company stock index 20 percent
- large cap company stock index 35 percent

You notice in the above stock allocation recommendation I call these various categories indexes. What is an index? A stock index is a mutual fund that tracks a specific market index like the S&P 500 Index or the Total Stock Market Index, for example. These mutual funds or ETFs try to match the performance of their index. There are many advantages in using an index fund/ETF, including the following:

✓ broader market exposure
✓ lower expenses
✓ low portfolio turnover
✓ passively managed

Here are some popular stock index funds and their market symbols:

- Vanguard Total Market Index Fund (VTI)
- Vanguard Small Cap Index Fund (VBK)
- Vanguard Mid-Cap Value Index (VMVIX)
- S&P Small Cap 600 Index (XSM)
- American Century Mid Cap Value Fund (ACMVX)
- Fidelity 500 Index Premium Class (FUSVX)
- S&P 500 Index (GSPC)

Unless you have professional training in finance and stock selection criteria, I do not recommend using individual stocks for your retirement funds. I prefer you to buy stock index funds, including ETFs.

My experience indicates many people are more familiar with the stock market than the bond market. Here are some very basic comments on bonds. Investors buy bonds because they produce steady income at relatively low risk. A bond's yield indicates how much income it will generate on an annual basis. This yield, derived by dividing the interest payment by the current price, falls as the price rises. (Basic math rules require as the denominator increases, the quotient of the equation decreases.) Bond yields also can tell us something about the future economy. Lower bond yields tend to forecast an expectation of a slower-growing economy in the future, and higher yields are forecasting a faster-growing economy.

Falling bond yields have been the primary direction of US markets since the high inflation days of 1981. The ten-year US Treasury note yield has fallen from 15.819 percent on September 30, 1981, to 1.366 percent on July 8, 2016.[1] Investment-grade corporate bonds typically have a higher yield than US government bonds.

I recommend the same approach for the bond or fixed income portion of your allocation process as I recommended for equities. Shy away from individual bonds. Bond index funds have the same advantages as stock index funds. Include both short-term and intermediate-term bond maturities while avoiding long-term bonds of more than five to seven years maturity. The names of bond index funds on this short list are considered conservative investments:

✓ Vanguard Total Bond Market Index Fund (VBMFX)
✓ Vanguard Short-Term Bond Index (VBISX)
✓ DFA One-Year Fixed Income (DFIHX)
✓ Fidelity Total Bond Fund (FTBFX)
✓ Barclay's US Aggregate Bond Index (SYBU)
✓ iShares Core US Aggregate Bond Fund (AGG)

One of the best reference sources I have found for investors who are not financial experts is Peter Mallouk's book *The 5 Mistakes Every Investor Makes and How To Avoid Them.* He discusses the importance of investors having a disciplined investment management approach. His recommendations could ultimately improve the probability of achieving

---

1   Ryan ALM.

investment goals. He has a proven track record of good investment performance while maintaining a long list of happy clients. He is a big fan of using ETFs to achieve your goals.

I also recommend maintaining a 5 percent cash position held in either a bank account or money market account with a mutual fund company. Having this cash reserve allows for greater flexibility by having ready access to some cash without selling any investments, if it is needed in an emergency.

You might be wondering why I have not recommended any international stock or bond exposure. Many financial advisers routinely recommend an international exposure of 10 to 20 percent of a total portfolio for a typical client. My personal preference is investments in companies with the bulk of their earnings coming from within the borders of the United States. Call me a contrarian in this regard or highly possessed by my home country bias. My basis for this position is all about risk management. In a recent study by S&P Dow Jones Indices sales in the United States accounted for approximately 44 per cent of the total for companies within the S&P 500, the rest coming from overseas. My premise is simply that most large cap US companies already have some portion of their earnings derived from overseas operations. For example, Coca-Cola, IBM, General Electric, Caterpillar, Apple, and Exxon Mobil, to name just a few, have significant international earnings. This provides more than enough international exposure for me by purchasing a stock or bond index fund that includes these and other large-cap US companies. I see no advantage in adding additional risk directly from fluctuating foreign exchange rates, foreign economic stability, and overall political risk to a portfolio. These are risks I do not have any expertise in evaluating, so I follow the simple rule of investing in companies I know and trust. To paraphrase Will Rogers, sometimes it is the return of the money that matters more than the return on it.

To further my thesis of sticking with what you know, here is additional evidence of how I achieve international exposure by investing in large-cap, US companies. According to the *Wall Street Journal*, as of year-end

2015, US companies had approximately $2.5 trillion in profits parked overseas. The reason these companies have chosen not to repatriate these profits back to the United States is because of our high corporate tax rate. Here are a few of those companies with the most earnings held abroad (all numbers are approximate estimates):

- Microsoft $105 billion
- General Electric $102 billion
- Apple $90 billion
- Pfizer $80 billion
- IBM $65 billion
- Merck $60 billion
- Alphabet $58 billion
- Johnson & Johnson $57 billion
- Cisco $56 billion
- ExxonMobil $50 billion

I may be a contrarian when it comes to adding international exposure to an investment portfolio, but I am more comfortable staying with companies that I know and trust rather than some nameless international index.

Key Components of the Planning Cycle

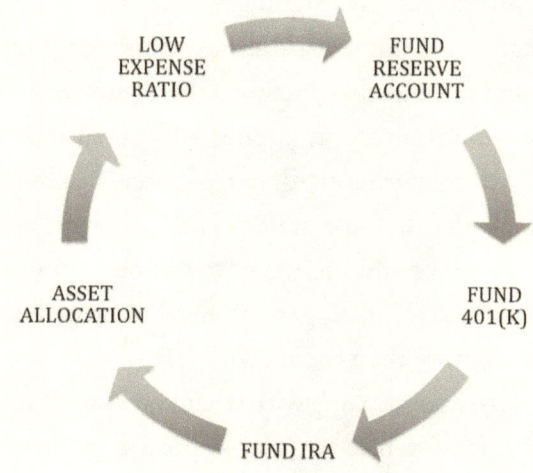

It is never as easy as "buy low, sell high." All investments have risk. The greatest risk, by far, is never taking one as it relates to investing for your retirement. I recommend you do your own research to find index funds/ETFS that you like. One of the most important considerations in choosing an index fund is the expense ratio. It is not uncommon to have an expense ratio below 0.10 percent ($10 per $10,000). The smaller the expense ratio, the more money invested and the better for you.

It is important to achieve diversification in your investment choices, as mentioned above. Too many people make developing a diversification strategy too difficult. The simple definition of diversification is to invest your assets in multiple segments of the markets to reduce risk. Following my overall investment philosophy, keeping things simple will usually result in the best results. Investors automatically achieve broad diversification in industries by investing in index funds or ETFs that follow a specific market index. I believe this is the most important element of diversification, not geography and not the various asset classes.

Looking backward where everyone has twenty-twenty vision, over the past eight years (March 2009–August 2016), foreign markets have underperformed US markets by a significant percentage. The SPX (S&P 500) had an annualized return of 19.37 percent, while the EFA (International ETF for Europe, Australia, and Far East) produced an annualized return of 11.88 percent versus the EEM (emerging markets), which came in at 9.98 percent per year. This is a significant difference in performance that makes a big difference in the growth of your retirement funds. Of course, past investment performance does not guarantee future results. My point is: do not overthink a diversification strategy. Keeping it simple, with an approach you understand and can explain to anyone asking about your strategy, should give you more peace of mind.

I believe index funds/ETFs give you the best chance for achieving overall investment success. As one of the greatest value investors, Benjamin Graham was quoted as saying, "The individual investor should act consistently as an investor and not as a speculator." Buying large, well-diversified stock and bond index funds/ETFs eliminates the gambler approach to investing.

Just like packing a suitcase in advance for a family trip, some preparation is required *before* beginning the process of executing your retirement plans. The better the preparation, the better the results of the plan. Having completed the initial requirements outlined in this chapter, it is now time to put them into action.

PART 2

EXECUTION

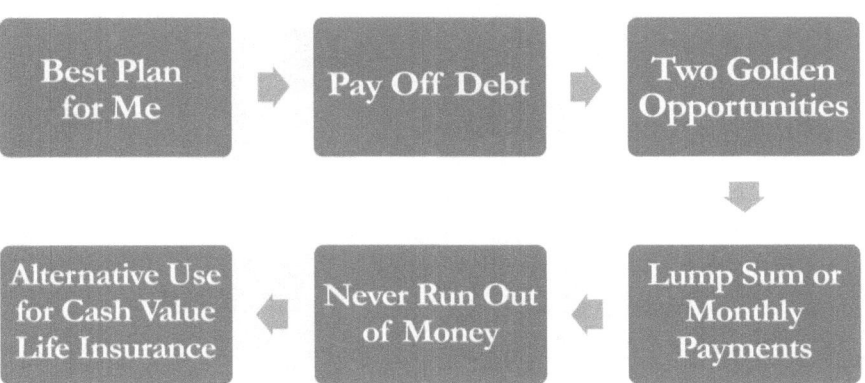

Chapter 6

....

What Is the Best Investment Plan?

Selecting investment products is all about understanding your level of risk tolerance. What do I mean by this? Finding your comfort zone for investing is the most important part of this process.

No one can predict the markets with any certainty. Investing involves risks, including the possible loss of principal, and investors should consider their personal circumstances carefully before investing. Wording like this appears on all investment brochures. It is the standard disclaimer to protect the investment company from future litigation. It can create enough fear and trepidation to scare off a seasoned investor. While all of us wish there was a totally safe investment for retirement, and if there were, none of us could afford that kind of total safety. We all need investments that have the potential for growth to overcome future inflation, taxes, and investment expenses. That reality leads us to consider making equity funds a permanent part of our retirement accounts.

The best investment plan is one you research and build from the available information. Do your due diligence. Separating all of the investment chatter into a working plan is not easy. In the previous chapter, I outlined some of the basic concepts to consider in constructing your personal plan. I do not stand in your shoes, and I cannot know your financial acumen or your risk tolerance.

If you are not comfortable making these initial decisions about your plan, then I do have a suggestion. I believe so strongly that at age fifty-five, you cannot wait any longer to catch up on your retirement funding, so I will give you a sample plan. Call it a default plan. It is a plan to move your retirement plans forward and from which you can build some self-confidence with your investment decisions.

A default retirement plan for catch-up funding should include these steps:

1. If you do not participate in an employer-sponsored plan, ask your employer when you can join the plan. If they do not have a plan, then you are on your own to build a default plan.

2. Open an online account with one of the retirement plan vendors, such as Fidelity, American Century, Charles Schwab, or Vanguard. If you are more comfortable doing this in person, each of these providers has fully staffed offices for this purpose in most major metropolitan areas. The employees are very helpful and can answer your questions and guide you in the account-opening process.

3. If you already have a 401(k) account or 403(b) account for public employees, just add additional funds to this account in the amount of your pay yourself first calculation. The same is true if you have an existing IRA. Adding to these existing accounts gets you started again.

4. If you are starting with a new account with a zero balance, then I suggest an asset allocation profile as follows:
   ¤ Equities 70 percent, (with small cap 15 percent, midcap 20 percent, and large cap 35 percent, all in index funds/ETF'S)
   ¤ Bonds or fixed income 25 percent (bond index funds)
   ¤ Cash reserves of 5 percent

Next, I would automate my monthly contributions through either a payroll deduction or an automatic bank transfer to my retirement trustee. Now you are on your way to achieving financial freedom in retirement.

If you still are not comfortable designing your do-it-yourself retirement plan or you do not like or trust my default plan, the only option left is to engage a financial adviser to do it for you. Hiring a financial adviser is serious business. You want to be very careful turning over all of your financial records to a stranger. You need to research financial advisers in your area; who do your most trusted friends use, and are they happy with the results? The financial adviser should have professional credentials such as a certified financial planner (CFP) or chartered financial analyst (CFA). You should meet with them in person, ask all the questions you can think of, fully understand how they bill for their services, and ask them to show you a sample quarterly report for a typical client. They should be able to explain everything in the quarterly report, line by line. One of the most important questions to ask is, "Are you working in a fiduciary role making sure whatever you recommend is in my best interest?" If the answer is no, move on. Typical fees are in the range of 1.0 percent per annum of assets under management (AUM). They usually bill quarterly. An account with an average $250,000 in total assets would receive a bill of $625 at the end of the quarter. Do not select a financial adviser who charges sales commissions or fees on the products they sell. They may find a way to sell you more products than you need. Would you ask a barber if you needed a haircut? *Never* engage with a financial adviser who cold calls you to sell you on his/her services. You need a personal reference from one or more satisfied clients to help you develop good chemistry with a financial adviser. After you have met with a potential adviser, if it does not feel right, then it probably is not the right adviser for you. Trust your instincts.

Hopefully these ideas will be the catalyst to get you started or restarted funding your retirement. Do not strive for absolute perfection in the design of your plan; eliminate the noise, and focus on making investment progress toward your financial goals, year after year. The best investment plan for you is one you are comfortable with and that moves you closer to your retirement goals over time. If you sleep well at night without worrying about your investments, then you have selected the best plan for you.

Here are my six recommendations for preparing a retirement plan:
1. Estimate your retirement income needs; plan to replace 100 percent of your preretirement income.

2. Do basic online research on your Social Security benefits; contact the Social Security administration for details, and review your annual Social Security statement.

3. Stay current on your employer's pension plan, 401(k) plan, or profit-sharing plan; track the value of your benefits; and understand the vesting schedule.

4. Contribute to tax-sheltered plans at the maximum dollar amount like 401(k)s and individual retirement accounts (IRA); your taxes will be lower. Understand any employer match, and take any balance in these accounts with you if you change jobs.

5. Leave retirement savings alone; do not borrow from any of these accounts. Continue making contributions until you reach full retirement age, at a minimum

6. Make a plan and make it happen, as success will come from execution.

Chapter 7

....

Pay off Debt

D rowning in debt? Is debt keeping you awake at night? Are you always making the minimum payment on your monthly bills? If you answer yes to any of these questions, you have a debt problem. Debt is a burden you need to eliminate before retiring. Paying off debt is the third component of a You-Centered Retirement Model.

Debt is as common as dirt because debt is as American as apple pie, Chevrolet, and baseball. Yes, debt in all its forms is easily available to all of us, and too much debt can be the result of some bad habits. Borrowing money for things we cannot immediately afford and putting the repayment schedule on an installment plan is how we have grown as a nation. If you currently have no debt, you are well ahead of most of your peers. Stay with your plan, and keep up the good work. Most of us, however, start our adult life with debt and keep adding to it over time. The most common types of debt are: home mortgage debt, auto loans, student loans, and credit card debt. Having debt is not the issue; learning how to manage it and ultimately become debt free is the challenge.

By age fifty-five, you should be well down the road to becoming debt free. You should know the difference between good and bad debt. You should only have good debt remaining on your balance sheet. Still not sure of the difference? Good debt is any debt that was borrowed to purchase an asset that will *appreciate* in value over time. An example of good debt is the mortgage on your home. Good debt can also be cheaper than bad debt because the US government offers a tax incentive or deduction for interest paid on a home mortgage, up to a maximum. In other words, interest paid on good debt is fully tax deductible. Bad debt is all other debt whose interest is not tax deductible. Student loan debt helped you prepare for a career with higher earning potential. It is good in that regard, but the interest paid on student loan debt is not fully tax deductible. The current limit for deductible interest is $2,500 per year, subject to income limits. Your adjusted gross income cannot be more than $80,000 for a single taxpayer or $160,000 for married filing a joint tax return. Debt on a car and credit card debt are for purchases that typically do not increase in value. These products tend to *depreciate* in value. So how are you doing in becoming debt free?

Credit Card Payments

Credit card debt is the most insidious type of debt because it always has high interest rates. These rates are also variable based on a factor above the bank prime rate. As the prime rate increases, so will your credit card interest rate. Typical interest rates on credit cards are double digits plus late fees and other charges. Whatever you do, make repaying all credit card debt first on your list so you can refocus on funding your retirement. A simple method to eliminate credit card debt involves these six steps:

- ✓ Stop all purchases using a credit card right away.
- ✓ Take all credit cards out of your wallet, and put them in a drawer, out of sight.
- ✓ Remembering the pay yourself first concept, take half of that monthly amount and apply it against your highest interest rate credit card.
- ✓ Continue this every month until all credit card balances have been fully repaid.
- ✓ Leave the credit cards in the drawer, and only pay cash for all purchases.

✓ Continue to fund your retirement accounts with the other half of the monthly pay yourself first amounts while you are paying off the credit cards.

This approach will return you to financial sanity. Any auto loan or student loan debt can be repaid following a similar approach. The point here is to get your finances back under control with only a home mortgage remaining as your primary liability.

Mortgage Payments

As there are only twelve years remaining before retirement in our example, you need a plan to accelerate mortgage payments if you want to achieve debt-free status by full retirement age of sixty-seven. The most common home mortgage term is a thirty-year mortgage. I do not recommend making payments for the full thirty years. To accelerate the payoff of the mortgage and reduce interest being paid to your mortgage lender, here is a repayment plan that will save you thousands in interest. Assuming you currently have a thirty-year mortgage with a fixed monthly payment, simply divide the monthly payment by two and pay this one-half of a mortgage payment every two weeks. The total paid for the month is the same dollar amount; just the timing of the payment is different. Remember the relationship between time and money? This is another example of that concept working in your favor. The mortgage companies dislike this repayment method because it lowers the amount of interest they earn from your mortgage. You will be the beneficiary of the savings because with this biweekly payment methodology, you will make twenty-six payments a year. That equates to one extra monthly payment annually (365 days divided by 14 days = 26 biweekly payments)!

Here is an example of putting this repayment approach into action: Assume a $100,000 mortgage at 5.0 percent on a fixed rate, thirty-year mortgage. The monthly payment is $536.82. Divide the monthly payment by two and the biweekly payment amount is $268.41. This biweekly payment method will generate the equivalent of one additional monthly payment every year with the same dollars. Using either payment method for a full year, the monthly plan payments total $6,441.84; the biweekly payment plan totals $6,441.84. The savings comes from a faster-reducing balance on which interest is charged.

Biweekly payment $268.41

Total number of years fifteen years

Total repaid $164,598.77

Total interest paid $64,598.77

Monthly payment $536.82

Total number of years thirty years

Total repaid $193,255.20

Total interest paid $93,255.20

Total savings using the biweekly payment method versus a standard monthly payment is $28,656.43 in interest. This is a meaningful amount of money that can be used to accelerate funding retirement accounts.

Paying off debt by full retirement age is a good thing. Being debt free in retirement eliminates one of the financial burdens many families face. Anything that contributes to a more worry-free retirement will be a factor contributing to your more positive attitude about life. Paying off debt is very straightforward. Make it happen.

Chapter 8

....

Two Golden Opportunities

T he earlier chapters in this book laid a foundation for understanding the need to focus on your retirement funding. Topics included pay yourself first, how to calculate personal net worth, the role of budgeting, goal setting, and the need to pay off debt. How to set up a plan has also been discussed. Helping you develop a comfort zone around retirement planning now leads to the most important aspects of implementing these plans. This chapter is the workhorse of *Time to Catch Up*. This is when you discover two golden opportunities to accelerate your retirement funding. This is the fourth strategy of a You-Centered Retirement Model.

The US government, through tax policy, subsidizes saving for retirement. The tax-deferred status of compounded earnings within retirement accounts like individual retirement accounts (IRAs) and 401(k) plans applies to all participants. This is the subsidy. Contributions to a 401(k) plan are also tax advantaged. Traditional IRA contributions may be tax deductible in the year made, if they are within the limits established for that year. In 2016, the adjusted gross income (AGI) limit for full deductibility was $61,000 for a single taxpayer and $98,000 for a joint tax filer, assuming both were also participating in an employer-sponsored plan. Without participating in such a plan, the AGI was $184,000 for both tax filers. A partial deduction is available for slightly higher AGI in each category. Roth IRA contributions are never tax deductible because they are made after-tax. However, here are the 2016

AGI limits to qualify for a Roth: $117,000 for single and $184,000 for joint tax filers. A Roth IRA has other advantages discussed later.

It is imperative to have both of these retirement accounts (IRA and 401(k)) if you are going to meet your retirement goals. If your employer offers a 401(k) or 403(b), you should participate. I recommend contributing the maximum allowed, which is $18,000 annually in 2016. If this number is too large, the minimum amount to be contributed should be the equivalent of any company match. Increase your contribution each year until you reach the maximum allowed.

Many companies offer a match in their 401(k) plans. A typical match might be 3.0 percent. This means at the end of the year, the company will add 3.0 percent of your gross salary to your 401(k) account, assuming you have contributed an equal or greater amount. This match is one of the only sources of *free money*. Do not miss this opportunity.

When the late Woody Allen suggested that 80 percent of success is just showing up, he was not referring to retirement planning. Just "showing up" by participating in a retirement plan will *not* be enough to achieve your retirement goals. If you are contributing 6.0 percent of your gross salary and the company offers a 3.0 percent match, your total contributions still total only 9.0 percent. This number needs to get to 15.0 percent, as soon as possible. Do whatever you can to raise your contribution level to the full 15.0 percent, with or without the company match.

In addition to the company 401(k) plan, you also should have either a traditional IRA or a Roth IRA. As long as you have earned income, you have these additional types of tax-advantaged options. I have already discussed the deductibility limits for a traditional IRA. In 2016 both types of IRA have the same $5,500 contribution limit. What are some of the differences?

A. Traditional IRA

   A traditional IRA may give you a tax deduction if you qualify. Adjusted gross income (AGI) up to $61,000 for an individual and $98,000 for a joint tax return are the current limits in 2016, assuming you are part of a plan. The limits are higher if you do not participate in such a plan. Even if your contributions are *not* tax deductible, this retirement product is worth having. Like most retirement accounts, compounded earnings are tax deferred. After age fifty-nine and a half, withdrawals are without penalties, but any withdrawal will be taxed as ordinary income. There are a few exceptions to this taxability, and they can be researched, if you are interested. After age seventy and a half, you can no longer make contributions to a traditional IRA, and you must begin to take required minimum distributions (RMD). The annual RMD is determined using an IRS actuarial table called the Uniform Distribution Table. It has different values for male and female account holders. You have a choice how to take the RMD: monthly, quarterly, annually, or some other combination. Failure to take the full RMD amount will result in a severe penalty. The RMD changes annually in accordance with the IRS actuarial table. Most traditional IRA accounts allow for loans to the account holder, under certain circumstances.

B. Roth IRA

The Roth IRA was created by the passage of the Taxpayer Relief Act of 1997, known as Public Law 105-34. It was named for its legislative sponsor, Senator William Roth of Delaware.

There is an AGI limit for qualification to make an annual contribution to a Roth IRA. AGI threshold amounts are for determining annual eligibility to contribute, not for eligibility to maintain a Roth IRA. In 2016 that limit is $117,000 for a single and $184,000 for a joint tax filer. If your AGI exceeds these limits, you will not qualify for a Roth IRA. The Roth IRA does not offer any tax deduction for contributions because they are made with after-tax dollars. After age fifty-nine and a half, withdrawals are tax-free. There are no required minimum distributions (RMD) with a Roth. You can continue to make contributions to a Roth as long as you have earned income. There are no taxes paid on Roth distributions after age fifty-nine and a half.

Funds held within a Roth IRA cannot be pledged as collateral for a loan under current IRS rules.

Either type of IRA is a good retirement product for most people. Anyone with earned income or who has a nonworking spouse can contribute to these accounts. The dollar limit on the contribution is either the amount of earned income or the stated maximum, whichever is less.

If your health permits and you choose to remain employed after age seventy and a half, you can continue to participate in an employer-sponsored Roth 401(k), regardless of age. The difference between this Roth 401(k) and a Roth IRA is in the RMD requirements. In a Roth IRA, there are no required minimum distributions (RMD). With a Roth 401(k), after age seventy and a half, RMDs will be required when you stop working and/or if you own 5 percent or more of the company. These rules can be complicated, and I encourage you to seek professional tax advice if this situation applies to you.

The good news about retirement funding does not stop here. There are even greater savings options with IRAs and 401(k) accounts than the basics outlined in the above paragraph. These are the two golden opportunities waiting to be discovered. I want you to seize these opportunities as soon as possible.

Seize These Opportunities Now

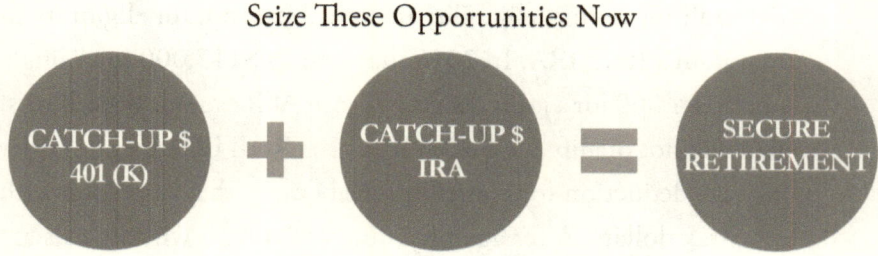

CATCH-UP $ 401 (K) + CATCH-UP $ IRA = SECURE RETIREMENT

A provision of the Economic Growth and Tax Relief Reconciliation Act of 2001 (EGTRRA) created a *catch-up* option for both 401(k) plans and IRAs alike. A *catch-up* provision is an elective deferral that is in excess of the statutory limit. The IRS sets the dollar amount of this catch up annually. Any individual who is age fifty or over at the end of the calendar year and who has earned income can make catch-up contributions. The Pension Protection Act of 2006 made catch-up contributions a permanent option in these retirement accounts. If you want to know more of the technical workings of these catch-up options, go to IRS.gov.

In 2016 the catch up amount for both types of IRAs was $1,000. This is in addition to the standard limit of $5,500. So in 2016, if you are age fifty or older, it is possible to contribute up to $6,500 annually to either type of IRA, using this catch-up option.

The catch-up amount for 401(k) accounts was $6,000 in addition to the standard limit of $18,000 in 2016. Thus a total contribution of $24,000 is possible using this opportunity. Now you see why I call these two catch up options golden opportunities? These are unique in the retirement field.

In 2004, the Vanguard Group conducted a study that found only 13 percent of eligible candidates use these catch-up options to expand their retirement savings. That means 87 percent of eligible account holders missed these opportunities! Earlier, I advised you to always maximize your savings in tax-deferred accounts. These golden opportunities provide you a way to accelerate funding your retirement accounts. You need to find the means, the dollars, to take advantage, if you want a fully funded retirement account at age sixty-seven.

By utilizing these catch-up provisions, you will accelerate achievement of your retirement goals discussed in chapter 1. Here are those original three examples illustrating the impact of the catch-up contributions on achieving the dollar goals:

- Assume you start with *zero* savings for retirement.

    Individual retirement account (IRA)—the catch-up provision is an extra $1,000 per year. With the same assumptions as the example in chapter 1, this $1,000 annually will be worth $19,141 in twelve years.

401(k) account—the catch-up provision is $6,000; this will have a future value in twelve years of $114,844.

Together these total $133,985.

With these catch-up contributions totaling $133,985, the remaining $440,234 needed to reach the goal of $574,219 will only require a monthly contribution of $2,000 compared to $2,500 without the catch-up amount. Total monthly contribution savings is $500. This level of contribution will create a total value of $583,790, an over-the-top funding of your goal.

- Assume you start with $50,000 in various retirement accounts.

  IRA—the extra $1,000 annually will become $131,750 in twelve years.

  401(k) account—the extra $6,000 per year becomes $227,453 in twelve years.

  Together these total $359,203.

  With these catch-up contributions totaling $359,203, the remaining $212,782 needed to reach the goal of $571,985 will require no additional contributions. In fact, this amount will grow to $696,400, a 22 percent over goal achievement!

- Assume you have $100,000 in retirement funds.

  IRA—the extra $1,000 annually becomes $244,360 in twelve years.

  401(k) account—the extra $6,000 annually has a future value of $340,063 in twelve years.

  Together these total $584,423.

  With these catch-up contributions totaling $584,423, there are no additional contributions needed to achieve the goal of $569,750. In fact, the goal has been overfunded by $14,673.

Taking full advantage of the catch-up contributions for both IRAs and 401(k) accounts dramatically increases the total account balances by exceeding the retirement goal in each example.

With a traditional IRA, Roth IRA, or 401(k) account, one of the forms required to be completed upon opening the account is a beneficiary designation form. Be sure to keep this designation current anytime changes are made to any retirement account. Upon your death, these retirement accounts will be transferred to the beneficiary shown on the designation. Your choice of beneficiary cannot be over ridden by a will or trust agreement. The beneficiary designation stands on its own merits. Keeping the beneficiary designation form current is your responsibility.

Let me make it even easier to visualize how you can catch up on funding your retirement accounts. In 2016 under the catch-up provisions for an IRA ($5,500 + $1,000 catch up) and a 401(k) ($18,000 + $6,000), if you were to contribute these maximum amounts each year for each retirement account, the total contributed in twelve years would be $366,000, without the effect of compound interest ($6,500 x 12 = 78,000 and 24,000 x 12 = 288,000 and the sum is 78,000 + 288,888 = 366,000). This is 92 percent of your total retirement goal! If you had just a small amount in each account prior to these catch-up years, you would be over the top in retirement funding. Now I know it is not easy to save $30,500 annually, but I did want to illustrate the retirement goal of $500,000 is within your reach, even if you are basically starting twelve years before your full retirement age.

How strong is your commitment to achieve a comfortable retirement? Take control of your retirement planning now to enjoy the benefits later. Success only comes from executing your plan. Again, I repeat, make a plan, and make it happen!

Chapter 9

....

Which Is Better: Lump Sum or Monthly Payments?

Any one of a number of major life events can occur throughout a career that may trigger the question: which is better—lump sum or monthly payments? This question centers on the decision you must make when changing jobs or changing career paths, or ultimately, when it is time to retire. Monies held in retirement accounts are portable. This means funds can be transferred from company-sponsored retirement plans or other IRA accounts when any of these events occur. The retirement monies can follow you to your new job or move to a self-directed IRA

Do not leave retirement funds with a previous employer *unless* you have a lifetime pension option under their plan. Otherwise, request these funds be issued to you or, better yet, transferred directly to another IRA trustee account. If the funds are issued to you, there is a sixty-day window to allow the reinvestment of these funds without penalty. This process is called an IRA rollover. Follow the specific rules for IRA rollovers to avoid taxation problems. See IRS.gov.

If you begin to withdraw funds from an IRA or 401(k) account before your age of fifty-nine and a half, these withdrawals become taxable. Additionally, you are subject to a 10 percent penalty tax for these early withdrawals. If you ask your employer to transfer funds out of your 401(k) account directly to you, the employer is required to withhold 20 percent for taxes on the transfer. A better way to transfer these retirement account dollars is to ask your employer to transfer them directly to another plan or to an IRA trustee in your name. No taxes are withheld on these types of transfers. Beware: the IRS allows only one rollover per year.

Some advantages of an IRA rollover include the following:

- lower costs
- more and better choices for investment
- *you* are in full control of the process

I saw a recent study confirming the average employee changes jobs seven times during his or her career. Again, my recommendation when you leave the employment of any company is to rollover your retirement account balances directly to an individual retirement account (IRA). The exception to this recommendation is if your previous employer offered a lifetime pension payout. In that case, you may choose to take advantage of the pension opportunity.

In my experience, most company retirement plans have limited investment options with relatively high expenses. This is because professional money managers who sell their plans to employers also design them and incorporate a higher fee structure. These plans usually include managed funds, which have active managers working to outperform the market. Fees for actively managed funds are higher than fees for passively managed index funds. By rolling over funds to your IRA, you have control of the funds, can find more suitable investment options, and can incur lower costs.

One last caution about the IRA-rollover process. Some employees borrow against their retirement accounts, and these loans should be repaid before transferring these accounts. Borrowing against retirement accounts is never encouraged; borrowing is a symptom of a lack of adequate reserve accounts to cover contingencies. Building a reserve account to cover six months of living expenses will allow you the flexibility to avoid borrowing against your retirement accounts.

The biggest advantage of a lump sum distribution over monthly payments is the continuity it can provide in continuing to build your retirement account balances. If the lump sum transfer acts as a bridge from your old company 401(k) account directly to a self-directed IRA, you have the advantage of having invested a larger sum in more suitable investment options at a lower cost. This is a win-win situation. It also will avoid any temptation by you of using these retirement funds for an interim purchase of something, with the best intentions of paying the funds back. If you never see the funds, you will be less inclined to want to spend them outside of your retirement account. Consider this an act of protection from any temporary lapse in your commitment to restoring your retirement funding priorities.

So will it be lump sum or monthly payments when you change employers? Make it a lump sum direct transfer to a self-directed IRA, and maintain your financial discipline toward achieving a comfortable, well-funded retirement.

Decision Time

Chapter 10

Never Run Out of Money

The fifth component of a You-Centered Retirement Model is making sure you never run out of money for as long as you live. Sound like a fairy tale or too good to be true? This is entirely possible.

Why not build your own pension plan when the paychecks stop? Social Security is one example of a lifetime annuity backed by the US government. See chapter 14 on integrating Social Security benefits. When you are ready to retire, buy yourself another type of annuity, a lifetime fixed immediate annuity with a portion of your retirement dollars, as a way to stretch your retirement dollars over your lifetime.

The good news about our advances in science, technology, and health care treatments is that, on average, we are living longer than previous generations. The bad news is a longer life could negatively impact your savings, lifestyle, and financial independence in those later years. Over 60 percent of retirees underestimate their life expectancy, according to the Society of Actuaries, 2011 Risks and Process of Retirement Survey. One simple solution to this problem is to purchase fixed immediate annuities. These insurance products, known as annuities, guarantee an income for your life, no matter how long you live. My recommendation is to consider the purchase of fixed immediate annuities after retirement. No medical history or medical exam is required.

The Society of Actuaries 2015 Risks and Process of Retirement Survey found that 85 percent of retirees would need to reduce spending significantly if they thought they were running out of money. After all, spending is the only variable they can control.

Here is an example how fixed immediate annuities work: Assume you are retirement age; you take $50,000 out of your retirement accounts to purchase a fixed immediate annuity with a ten-year guarantee. You will begin receiving a monthly check shortly after you purchase the annuity. This monthly check amount will be the same for the rest of your life. The amount does not fluctuate. Even after the total payouts exceed your purchase price of $50,000, you will continue to receive the fixed monthly payment. The quoted payout rate includes both interest and return of premium.

The total payments received may be more or less than what you paid, depending on how long you live. People with longevity on their side, hopefully, will collect more than they paid. What about someone who dies shortly after he or she purchases the fixed immediate annuity? With a ten-year guarantee feature, if you die before the ten years have passed, your beneficiary will receive the remaining payments during the ten-year guarantee period. This is a simple explanation of a fixed immediate annuity. These products can become more complicated, with many different options. Consult with your insurance agent or financial adviser before taking final action.

There are several different ways to pay for this product. You can take money out of a checking or savings account, called nonqualified money, or transfer funds from one of your retirement accounts, called qualified money. Taking funds out of your retirement account bond or fixed income allocation to buy an immediate annuity is my choice. I recommend no more than 20 to 25 percent of these funds be used for an immediate annuity. By funding the annuity in this manner, you have not lowered your total retirement accounts; you have just reallocated a portion of them to the annuity.

Do not forget your spouse when it comes to purchasing an immediate annuity. Actuarial tables show that women, on average, live longer than men. Your female spouse can expect to spend five to ten years as a widow. Not to be gruesome, but that is just a fact. If you are married, I recommend purchasing an immediate annuity with a 100 percent joint and survivor life income, meaning you will receive a lifetime income, and upon your death, your spouse will receive an income for her remaining life as well. Upon the death of the second person, all payments cease.

Research annuities online at ImmediateAnnuities.com, or talk with either your life insurance agent or a financial adviser about how to purchase this longevity insurance. Annuities are contracts with insurance companies and can provide a guaranteed lifetime income stream. The purchase of an immediate annuity requires a lump sum payment. The monthly income can be for life or for a fixed period of time, with a lifetime provision. Look into the ten-year certain fixed period as an attractive option.

Here are some of the advantages of immediate annuities:

- They provide regular, monthly income.
- Payments are taxable but at a lower tax because of an exclusion ratio. Each payment is considered to include some portion of the original principal contributed, and only the remaining portion of the payment is taxed. (The principal portion is excluded from taxation as part of the exclusion ratio. Once the cost basis is recovered, the entire payment amount becomes taxable.)
- Some states will allow immediate annuities to be exempt from creditors. Check with your state of residency for the details that apply to you.
- Immediate annuities offer a better payout ratio than most conventional investments, like bank certificates of deposit, savings accounts, and money market mutual funds.

Everything is not perfect regarding immediate annuities. They are not for everyone. Here are some of the common disadvantages:

- They lack liquidity. Once you make a lump sum payment, you have given up any control over those funds. This is an irrevocable contract.
- They pay a fixed amount of money, based on the particular contract you have entered into with the insurance company. Therefore, they offer no protection from future inflation.
- They are not FDIC insured like most bank products.
- On average, annuity returns are less than the historical returns for the stock market.
- You run the risk of dying early, and if you chose the lifetime payment option, there will be no funds transferred to your estate. The insurance company keeps any funds left after your death. They win; you lose. There are ways to avoid this, but each of these options will cost more money in the form of reduced payouts.

Remember—immediate annuities are a contract with an insurance company. It is an irrevocable transaction once the insurance contract has been delivered to the buyer. One risk every annuity owner assumes is the future financial stability of the company issuing the annuity. I recommend you only buy an immediate annuity from an insurance company with an A.M. Best rating no lower than an A to A++. This rating is not a guarantee of the solvency of the company, but it does indicate the company has undergone a rigorous financial review to obtain this rating. The highest rating possible from A.M. Best is A++. A.M. Best Co. is the oldest insurance rating agency in the world. They have been reporting on the financial condition of insurance companies since 1899. Other rating services you might consider are Moody's Investor Service, with their highest rating of Aaa, Standard & Poor's rating of AAA, and Fitch's rating of AAA, which is also their highest rating. All guaranteed payments under these insurance contracts are subject to the claims-paying ability of the issuing insurance company.

If immediate annuities can do all of these positive things in retirement, why not put all my retirement dollars into immediate annuities? Absolutely *not*! You need to maintain diversification of the investments in your retirement funds. Immediate annuities can represent a portion of how you allocate these funds, but only a portion. Again, I recommend no more than 20 to 25 percent of your bond allocation be used to purchase an immediate annuity. I also have recommended you maintain a cash reserve balance of at least six months' equivalent of your living expenses for emergencies. Other than immediate fixed annuities, I would avoid all other types of annuities.

Maintaining liquidity and control of your retirement funds is vitally important. None of us has a clear crystal ball foretelling the future. Things happen, and we change our minds many times about our priorities in life. Maximum flexibility with your retirement funds gives you one more element of control for your ultimate peace of mind.

Creating your own pension plan with the purchase of an immediate annuity gives you an assurance of never running out of money during your lifetime. Annuities are a form of longevity insurance, not an investment. The purpose of an immediate annuity is to generate income during retirement. I repeat, they are not considered an investment option. Consider these insurance products as only one of the multiple components of your retirement plan.

One note of caution: with today's low interest rates, now is not a good time to lock in a fixed payment for the rest of your life. One possible solution is to build an annuity ladder. Consider spreading out the purchase dates of several annuities over the next five to six years. Remember—I am recommending investing no more than a total of 20 to 25 percent of the fixed income allocation of your retirement accounts. Look at buying the first annuity now (one-third of the dollar amount allocated for annuities) and then the second and third annuity each of the next two to three years. You will have invested the same amount of money as your initial annuity allocation. The payouts will be higher because you are older, and they will increase, if interest rates rise over that time period. Low interest rates equate to low payouts because the insurance companies earn less on their investments. Also spread the risk by purchasing each annuity from a different insurance company.

Chapter 11
....

Alternative Use for Cash Value Life Insurance

One of the often-overlooked sources of additional money for retirement funding can be found in cash value life insurance policies (CVLI). There are various types of CVLI policies like whole life and some universal life policies. If you own only term insurance policies, which have no cash value, you can stop reading the rest of this chapter, unless you are uninsurable and your term policy is still convertible to whole life. This discussion will focus only on whole life insurance policies with cash value.

This is *not* a chapter arguing against whole life insurance policies. They can provide a constant level of protection throughout your life, at a fixed premium. The premium is typically lower than what a new policy would cost because the whole life policy was purchased when you were younger. I personally own some whole life policies. I do not advocate the wholesale cash out of any or all of your whole life policies. The ownership of life insurance is a very personal decision. If you own life insurance, you have made these purchases because the insurance products offered solutions to particular financial concerns you had when the policies were purchased. Protection against your untimely death is one of the most common reasons to own life insurance. Providing financially for a growing family is a major responsibility that can be transferred to life insurance upon your death. Funding a trust for your estate may be another reason. There can be many variations of these and other reasons, as well. Whatever you want to accomplish with life insurance is a matter of personal choice. I do know that once you have determined your need for insurance coverage, the amount and type of insurance should be consistent with your personal goals and dreams and the overall needs of those who depend on you for financial support.

What I am suggesting is that you should review your life insurance coverage from time to time, as the need for insurance may have changed over the past twenty years. Also be sure to review your beneficiary designations, as well as the ownership of the policy. If someone other than yourself owns the policy on your life, you want to be sure there is a contingent owner to this contract, in the event that original owner dies before you do. Your children may be grown, living on their own, and pursuing their careers independent of you and your spouse. Time, hard work, and the pursuit of a frugal lifestyle may have provided you the opportunity to build other assets that can now be used to mitigate some of the need for life insurance from an estate perspective. Single people, widows, and widowers who have no financial dependents may choose to stop paying life insurance premiums, cash out the available cash value, and use this extra money to invest for retirement. This is a *really big decision,* and it should not be undertaken lightly.

By all means, if you are in poor or declining health, *do not spend any time thinking about accessing cash value in life insurance policies.* Keep the policies in force to provide a death benefit for the beneficiaries. Your heirs will be appreciative. Be very cautious about making any changes if you are no longer insurable.

What is the difference between face value and death benefit in a life insurance policy? Face value is the dollar amount of the insurance contract you initially purchased. For example, if you purchased a whole life $100,000 face value policy, paid your premiums on time, and did not violate any of the requirements of the policy during your lifetime, the face value is still $100,000. The death benefit is the actual dollar amount paid by the insurance company upon your death, assuming you are the insured. In this example, the death benefit could be the same as the face value, or it could be different. If your policy was a participating policy sold typically by a mutual insurance company and it paid annual dividends, the use of those dividends could affect the value of the death benefit. If the dividends were used to purchase additional paid-up insurance, the death benefit will be *higher* than the face value. If the dividends were used to lower the premiums, the death benefit *will be the same* as the face value. If loans were taken against the cash value and never fully repaid, or cash withdrawals were utilized, the death benefit *will be lower* than the face value. I know it may sound confusing, but the details are always the most important part of any insurance contract.

As illustrated in the paragraph above, death is not a requirement to access cash value in a whole life policy. Most of these policies allow for either cash withdrawals and/or loans against the accumulated cash value. Read the policy for specific details on this process or contact your insurance agent for assistance.

The insurance company will automatically provide an annual statement summarizing the policy you have purchased. These come to you by regular mail, so pay attention to correspondence received from your insurance company. This is a general report that will give the basic up-to-date information about the policy. A more meaningful and detailed report on the status of the policy is called an in-force policy illustration. You must request the in-force policy illustration, but it is a free report. You will be able to see if and when the policy will lapse, if that event is projected to occur anytime during the life of the policy. Use this information to keep up to date with the details of each life policy. If you have questions on either of these reports, contact your insurance agent.

What is a classic surrender squeeze? This is a term used by financial advisers and insurance analysts. As the insured, you could be required to surrender a life insurance policy if one of the following three events were to occur:

- excessive loans and accrued interest against a policy not repaid
- cash withdrawals in a universal policy that depletes internal cash
- very low investment gains in a universal policy

The solution to this squeeze is threefold:

- Repay policy loans or replace cash withdrawals (rebuild the cash).
- Increase annual premiums to cover additional cash needs within the policy.
- Let the policy lapse or surrender it to the insurance company, as it has no value.

How can a whole life policy lapse? You thought it was for life when you purchased it.

To avoid whole life policies from lapsing, the premiums must be paid on time and loans should also be repaid in a timely manner. A minimum level of cash must be maintained within the policy. The cash level inside the policy is critical, as the insurance company taps into this cash each year to cover the policy's internal costs. This can include unpaid premiums being deducted from the cash, which creates an automatic loan that will accrue interest. This policy provision is called coverage protection guarantee. If the cash level drops too low, the policy can lapse.

If you decide to cancel a policy and withdraw the cash value, beware of potential tax implications. If the policy is worth less than the total premiums paid, the conversion of the cash value could be tax-free. However, if the loans plus interest or cash withdrawals exceed the amount of paid premiums, you could be taxed on the difference at ordinary income tax rates. I recommend you consult with your tax professional as policies that lapse can have tax consequences.

If the annual premium is too costly for your budget in preretirement or postretirement, and you still need insurance coverage, consider one of these solutions:

- Use the cash value of the policy to buy a reduced, paid-up contract.
- Change the use of any dividend to apply toward the reduction of annual premiums.

If you are still looking for additional income, consider cashing out the policy and saving the annual premium. If you still need insurance coverage, follow one of the solutions shown above.

Keep all of your life insurance policies together in a safe place like a safety deposit box or home safe. This will make it easier for your heirs when it is time to file a death claim under the insurance policy.

You bought whole life insurance for the purpose of protection for a lifetime, not as an investment. I do not think life insurance is the best investment vehicle. There are better investments available, as discussed in chapter 5.

From this brief discussion, I hope you understand the importance of life insurance policies; however, they should be reviewed from time to time for their relevance to your current circumstances. There may be no reason to make changes, but maybe there is. Life insurance may not be necessary forever, as you originally thought.

The various alternative ways to use CVLI life insurance policies to enhance retirement funding can be summarized as follows:

- Continue paying premiums and keep things as they are.
- Cancel the policy and use the cash to supplement retirement.
- Keep the face amount the same but redirect the dividend to supplement retirement.

Take a reduced paid-up policy to free up cash flow.

Having invested your time and money in this book, the next step is to do something with the knowledge you are acquiring from *Time to Catch Up*. If you can execute on some or all of these strategies, you should be capable of becoming financially independent in retirement. This peace of mind is worthy of your *best effort*.

PART 3

LIVING THE DREAM

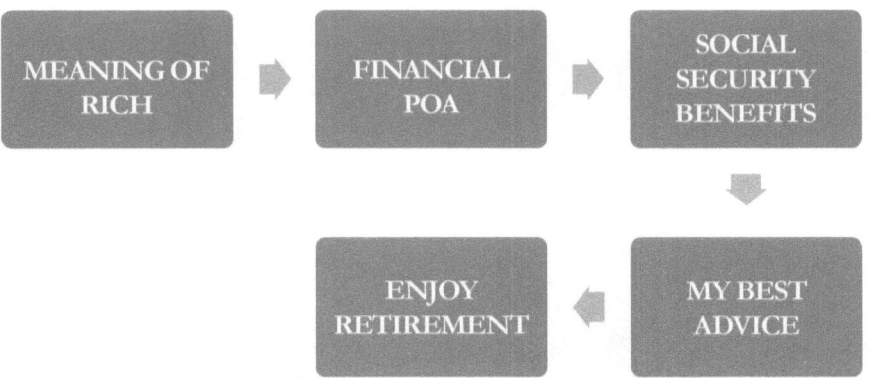

Chapter 12

....

What Does It Mean to Be Rich?

Growing up in a small midwestern town had a lot of advantages. It was safe, I knew most of the people, and they knew my parents or me. Most people were empowering and supportive of any community activity. They offered encouragement and advice when I tried something new. It was easy to identify the rich from the not-so-rich. The rich drove newer cars, lived in bigger houses, and dressed well. All of these were external factors I thought defined well-to-do or rich people. I was confident I knew what to look for in describing someone as rich. As I grew into adulthood, my definition and understanding of rich changed dramatically.

Looking rich versus being rich. This is the bottom line and what I ultimately came to realize was my misdirected childhood criteria in deciding who was rich and who wasn't. Remember the book *The Millionaire Next Door?* The central thesis was that you cannot tell by outward appearances who is rich and who isn't, even on a strictly financial basis. I am reminded of the man who lived in the same house his entire life, having taken care of his ailing parents until their deaths. He had never married, and most of his friends were work related. He worked hard every day, wore work clothes his entire life, and drove a truck that had seen better days ten years before. His was a comfortable lifestyle, but without all the frills and extras we have come to expect, if not demand. He had one television, and his entertainment beyond the TV was spending time with family members and discussing the current events of the day. Upon his death, I was appointed by the court as one of his representatives to settle his estate. What a surprise to discover this man had accumulated a sizable estate. His instructions were simple and straightforward with how he wanted his estate distributed. I followed his directions exactly and settled his estate well within the allotted time by the probate court. This man could have been the poster person for *The Millionaire Next Door*. I learned a life-changing lesson.

Time to Catch Up is about building an investment plan for achieving financial independence in retirement. It is not a spiritual discussion on the meaning of life or creating a lifestyle for the rich and famous. I do believe each of us has a need to develop our personal relationship with God and church on terms we are comfortable. I will not dwell on religion, as that is not the focus of this book.

I am asked frequently if following a You-Centered Retirement Model will lead to people becoming rich. I have struggled with developing a coherent answer to this question. It really depends on what you mean by rich. What I do know is that the tongue-in-cheek aphorism that "whoever dies with the most toys wins" is a very superficial comment on life.

Many people still think in terms of how much money has been saved and invested as the primary definition of being rich. I am not of this school of thought. I view money as a means to an end. Yes, money can provide for a comfortable living, pay for an education for your children, and generate sufficient retirement benefits for you and your spouse. All of these are important; however, for me, it is equally important to keep money in perspective.

Money, as defined by your personal net worth, is not the same as self-worth. Self-worth can be enhanced by net worth but not supplanted by it. I believe each of us should take pleasure in what we have achieved and the lifestyle it can offer. This can include positive reflections on career accolades, raising independent and self-sufficient children, maintaining a loving and respectful relationship with your spouse throughout a marriage, and nurturing the person we have become rather than dwelling on what we used to do to earn a living. Are we to be defined by what we do or by who we are?

John Bogle, founder and former CEO of the Vanguard Mutual Fund Group and the creator of the first index mutual fund, wrote a book entitled *Enough*, which talks about the true measures of money, business, and life. I will paraphrase him from that book in which he asks the question "Should we measure ourselves by what we have or by what we are (our character)?" This is the essence of what I believe is really important in life: being close to family, having friends to share experiences, and being happy we can do what we want, when we want, and with whomever we want to spend the time. This is my definition of being rich.

This book is about making a transformation of your financial life. It is a step-by-step approach in developing a plan to achieve a specific retirement goal. If these strategies are implemented successfully, they can provide adequate funding to support a comfortable and sustainable retirement.

How much is enough? When John D. Rockefeller was asked how much was enough, he answered, "Just a little more." I prefer my version of John Bogle's philosophy that enough saving for retirement is when we feel empowered to live our lives on the basis of who we are, not how much we have! In retirement enough does not have to mean more. I have learned to be happy with what I have. I am no longer in the relentless pursuit of more. This has brought about a calming sense of acceptance of where I am in life.

Research studying the correlation between money and happiness has developed some interesting conclusions. One of the most prominent conclusions is that *experiences* tend to provide more lasting happiness than material things. Your life is full of experiences, and your photo album has probably captured many of them for posterity. Continue to enjoy those experiences and interact with life. Do not cut off this source of ongoing pleasure just because you are preparing for retirement or even during retirement. The best of life is not just measured in dollars and cents. It is all the little things that really matter. Several years ago, the song "My Own Little World" was written by Matthew West as an anthem of encouragement to get out of ourselves and "our own little world." It resonates perhaps even more today.

Albert Schweitzer defined a successful life as follows: "Success is not the key to happiness. Happiness is the key to success." Enough said.

Chapter 13

....

Why You Need a Financial Power of Attorney

The need for a financial power of attorney (POA) is the sixth component of a You-Centered Retirement Model. Before I describe this legal document, let's discuss a more commonly known form of a power of attorney covering your personal health care.

While all of us hope to live to a ripe old age, maintaining good health and retaining our mental capacity, the growing population within assisted living and nursing home facilities projects that not all of us can expect to reach old age on such good terms. To assist us in decision-making in our older years, we have become accustomed to the need for a durable power of attorney (POA) for health care.

What is a durable power of attorney for health care? It is a legal arrangement to name someone else to assume responsibility for making health care decisions for you when you are no longer capable of making such decisions. It is a formal, legal document. It provides you the opportunity to name a trusted person to step into your shoes when the time comes. Your ability to make good decisions can be impacted by old age, dementia and other illnesses, a stroke, or some other form of mental impairment. Good examples of persons named to act on your behalf might include your spouse, your children, or a trusted adviser, such as an attorney or any other person in whom you have confidence. The point is that *you* make the selection of whom you want named as your agent in the durable power of attorney (POA).

Not only does the durable power of attorney for health care provide you the opportunity to name an agent to make decisions for you, the POA can also outline what you want done in certain medical emergencies. A *do not resuscitate* (DNR) provision may also be included. This gives clear instructions to the medical staff what you want done, if you are not able to communicate with them because of a serious medical condition. This is a real life-or-death document.

The term *durable* means the document stays in effect if you become incapable for any reason. If you never need the POA, it will just yellow with age in a file somewhere.

A durable power of attorney for health care is a *must* document. You need to talk with an attorney and complete this form as soon as possible.

A durable power of attorney for financial matters is lesser known but of equal importance. While it does not concern matters of life or death, it performs a similar service as the durable power of attorney for health care. What happens if your mind is not as sharp as it was when you put together your plan for retirement? How do you protect yourself and your family from mistakenly mismanaging your affairs due to mental impairment? A financial POA is not just for those who suffer dementia or a serious stroke. When you grant someone a durable POA for financial matters, he or she takes on the fiduciary responsibility for protecting your assets and income sources.

Naming a trusted person or agent in this POA is equally as important as in the health care POA. The same list of trusted persons might be considered, as well as a CPA or other financial adviser familiar with your financial affairs. Whomever you select needs to be fully aware of all of your financial matters. You should arrange an appointment periodically to keep this person current on your finances.

A durable power of attorney for financial matters can free you from worry about money decisions in the future. You can voluntarily turn over your assets and income sources to your selected agent at any time to manage them on your behalf. The other option is to turn over control of your financial life *only* if you are declared incompetent. The ultimate decline in your state of mind can also give you some current peace of mind that you have addressed the potential of this outcome.

You need to protect yourself and your family against a failing ability to judge risks adequately as you get older. It would be a shame to make some poor money decisions that destroy your financial wellbeing in your later years. Hopefully you will never need to activate a durable power of attorney for financial matters because you remain capable of managing your affairs until death.

A third legal document of importance is a living will. By the age of fifty-five, you should have addressed this necessity and already have one on file with your legal papers or tucked inside a safety deposit box. If you do not have one, now is the time to meet with an attorney and complete this task.

A will can be much more than just another legal document. A will can be simple or complex, depending on your requirements. For a will to be recognized as valid, it must meet certain legal requirements. A will may include the following:

- naming of an executor to be responsible for administering the disposition of your estate
- specific instructions on the distribution of your property to your heirs
- naming of a guardian for any minor children
- creation of testamentary trusts as part of your overall estate plan

A living will is your written instructions on how you want assets held in your name distributed after your death. You may have an antique rocker received as a gift from your grandmother that you want to pass on to your daughter. There may be other tangible items like jewelry, art, baseball player cards, the family Bible, a box of love letters between your mother and father, family photo albums, and many other things that have a very special meaning to you. The living will can carry out your instructions on the disposition of these items after your death.

A living will can also name a guardian for your minor children, if you are no longer around to provide for them. This decision to name a guardian is important both in the event of your death and any time you travel outside the country. You should get the approval of whomever you name before you include them in your will. They need to be willing guardians when the time comes.

A living will should include instructions for assets in your name only. Assets held in joint name will usually pass automatically to the jointly named party. You cannot pass along life insurance proceeds by way of a will, as life policies have a designated beneficiary. The beneficiary will receive the proceeds directly from the insurance company. Likewise, individual retirement accounts (IRA) and 401(k) accounts have named beneficiaries, as well. These retirement balances will pass along to the beneficiaries and cannot be redirected by a will.

Finally, a living will means just that; it can be changed any time up until your death, assuming you are of sound mind. The living will is not effective until your date of death. Keep it current with your wishes and updated with any change in taxation laws by meeting with your estate-planning attorney from time to time.

The need for both a durable power of attorney for health care and a separate one for financial matters should be a priority. Do this for both yourself and your family. These legal arrangements are all about *your* quality of life. All of your plans, hopes, and dreams for retirement can change in an instant due to an accident or serious illness. These legal declarations allow you to remain in full control of your future wellbeing, including both health care and financial matters, by *you* making the decision on whom to name as a trusted agent. Why let a court or some other entity decide who should be your guardian and assume responsibility for your medical or financial decisions? Naming a trusted agent to look after you in matters of health care and finance just makes sense.

Chapter 14

....

How to Integrate Social Security Benefits

Like a lot of people nearing retirement age, I had not spent much time learning about Social Security, its myriad rules, and their impact on benefit calculations until I was ready to retire. This was a mistake, and I do not want you to make the same one. A lack of knowledge can cost you a lot of money in retirement. Appreciating how Social Security works and integrating it into your overall retirement plan is the seventh and final strategy of a You-Centered Retirement Model. Let me start the discussion about Social Security with a summary on the source of taxes funding your federal retirement account.

The tax funding the Old Age, Survivors and Disability Insurance (OASDI) and Medicare (Hospital Insurance) (HI) is collected for employees under the Federal Insurance Contributions Act (FICA) and for self-employed individuals under the Self-Employment Contributions Act (SECA). The total dollar amount collected is the same for both types of employees, but under FICA the tax is paid equally between employer and employee (half for each). The current tax rate for Social Security is 6.2 percent paid by the employee and another 6.2 percent paid by the employer. This total Social Security tax of 12.4 percent is applied on income up to $118,500 annually. The tax for OASDI applies only to earned income up to the wage base established each year. No limit applies to earnings for the tax for HI. The 2016 wage base for OASDI for both employee and self-employed is the same: $118,500. However, the tax rate for HI is 1.45 percent for employee, 1.45 percent for employer, and 2.95 percent for self-employed. Again, there is no wage limit on calculating the HI tax.

Eligibility for full coverage under Social Security is a minimum of 40 quarters (10 years) of earned income, where some amount of OASDI tax has been paid. The federal government tracks this information from your annual tax return. The full retirement age to collect full benefits is age sixty-six in 2016 for persons born 1943 till 1954. Full retirement age for a person currently fifty-five years of age is sixty-seven (birth years 1960 and later). Please refer to SocialSecurity.gov for answers to all of your questions regarding Social Security.

The earliest you can draw on your Social Security account is age sixty-two. The benefit at this early age is discounted by 25 percent from what you will receive at full retirement age. If you are not in good health, have a family history of premature death, or just really need the money, drawing Social Security at age sixty-two may be the best option you have. Everyone has their unique family history and set of circumstances; therefore, you are the only one who can make this decision. If you decide to begin drawing on your Social Security at age sixty-two, I want you to have full knowledge of what you are giving away.

In addition to the penalty for tapping Social Security early (25 percent discount in benefits), there is also a reduction in benefits based on a wage base above $15,720. If you are drawing Social Security before your full retirement age, one dollar of benefits is withheld for $2 in earned income above $15,720. It is possible to recover this withholding in additional benefits, if you live long enough. To be more specific: if you file a joint federal tax return and if your combined income is below $32,000, none of your Social Security benefits are taxable. If the combined income totals $32,000 to 44,000, as much as 50 percent of your benefits are subject to tax. If your combined income exceeds $44,000, then 85 percent of the benefits are subject to tax. The tax applied will be your tax bracket calculated by AGI plus nontaxable interest and one-half of your

Social Security benefits. Consult your tax professional for guidance in this difficult area of taxation.

How many times would you knowingly walk away from a 24 percent increase in annual benefits? That is what everyone does if they chose to begin Social Security payments at sixty-seven, your full retirement age in our example. If you can wait until age seventy, the benefits will increase 8.0 percent each year. This can represent a substantial increase in your lifetime payments from Social Security. This is one example of maximizing your Social Security benefits. Most people chose the benefits that are payable at their full retirement age. This is the highest level of benefits available without delaying beyond your full retirement age.

Here are the maximum monthly benefits available from Social Security in 2016:

Full Retirement Age (FRA)	$2,639 (the average monthly payout for all retirees is $1,342)
Begin Drawing at Age Sixty-Two	$2,102 or a 26 percent reduction from FRA
Wait till Age Seventy	$3,576 or a 36 percent increase from FRA

The basic question some people ask when considering what age to begin drawing Social Security is, "What is the break-even for early versus delayed Social Security benefits?" Or is less money now better than more later? The answer is, it depends.

The longer you live, the better it is to delay taking Social Security. This is called longevity. Who knows how long they will live? Fortunately, the Social Security Administration has developed longevity tables to assist in this analysis. A male at age sixty-five is projected to live an average of another sixteen years (age eighty-one); a female age sixty-five is projected to live an average of another nineteen years (age eighty-four). Your family history will be important in how you apply these longevity tables. Because of so many variables with each person's life, the Social

Security Administration has removed the break-even analysis calculator from their website. The best rules of thumb indicate the following:

1. If you begin to draw Social Security benefits more than three years before your full retirement age (FRA), an approximate break-even would be twelve years (144 months) after you reach FRA.

2. If you begin less than three years before FRA, the approximate break-even is fifteen years (180) months after you begin receiving benefits. Note that these two break-evens are the same; twelve years after reaching FRA (67 + 12 = 79) and fifteen years after starting to receive benefits (64 + 15 = 79) equates to the same number of years for an approximate break-even.

For more examples on break-even analysis regarding when to begin taking Social Security benefits, Google Social Security break-even analysis.

Social security is another form of longevity insurance, backed by the US government and its benefits are adjusted annually by a cost of living (COLA) factor. The COLA is intended to maintain your Social Security benefits purchasing power consistent with the annual inflation rate. This is also a form of annuity, and you may want to refer to chapter 10, where I discussed other forms of immediate payment annuities.

I am frequently asked, "What is the best Social Security strategy for me?" I hate to say it, but again, it depends. The answer depends on your individual situation. I have outlined a few of the options available for persons approaching retirement age. This is not an exhaustive listing. I hope you have gained an appreciation for the complexity of the Social Security system from these limited comments. I recommend when you are ready to seriously consider accessing your Social Security benefits, schedule a face-to-face appointment with your local Social Security office. I have found these representatives to be knowledgeable and helpful in answering your specific questions and guiding you through the application process. Just remember—full retirement age (FRA) depends on your birth year:

- born between 1943 and 1954 = FRA is 66
- born 1960 and after = FRA is 67

For complete details about full retirement age determinations, go online to www.SocialSecurity.gov.

One of the biggest surprises for me in retirement has been in the area of expenses. All of the literature I had read projected how expenses should decrease in retirement. I have not found that to be the case with me. I think our increased travel and more frequent eating out expenses are probably the culprit. Anyway, it is for this reason I recommend you plan to replace 100 percent of your preretirement income. Make room in your budget for more contingencies because they just seem to always pop up.

More senior citizens receive Social Security than monies received from all other forms of longevity insurance. Social Security is one of your most valuable retirement assets. As a result, I believe it is critical for you to understand the basics of how it works and what some of the options are, if you choose to maximize your benefits. Whether you maximize your Social Security benefits or not, I want you to know how much money you potentially leave on the table with your decision on when to draw benefits. With this information, you are making a fully informed decision when you decide at what age to begin to draw your Social Security benefits. This decision is one of the most important you will make about retirement, as it affects the total dollar amount of benefits received for the rest of your life. Social security benefits are only one leg of my four-legged retirement income stool. Their value and importance, however, is more than 25 percent of the total value of your potential total retirement package.

Chapter 15

A Review of My Best Advice

This book has discussed seven powerful strategies on how to accelerate funding for your retirement accounts. Why not just skip the rest of the book and focus on this chapter, which includes my best advice? Could this chapter be the equivalent of the CliffsNotes version of *Time to Catch Up*? No, it is not. If you do not understand the interrelationship of the seven strategies of a You-Centered Retirement Model, you miss the whole point of retirement planning. You also might miss the opportunity to begin earning investment returns today that may accelerate growth in your retirement accounts in later years. Consider reading this entire book as one way to expand your financial literacy. Do not skip the rest of the book; refer back to it often to answer your questions, now and in the future.

There are many books, articles, TV shows, and seminars that give financial advice about retirement. Each of them may offer some very good insights that can assist you in the development of a plan. The key takeaway from all of them is that you need a plan! When you enter the decade of your fifties, it is time to reassess your current retirement situation and formulate a retirement strategy. This plan must be based on reality. You are beyond the era of expecting a "gold watch" retirement party when you leave your career and immediately enter retirement. We live in a rapidly changing world because of technology, social media, and the shifting demographics of how different age groups impact our economy. Rapid change translates into the need for a backup plan when plan A no longer is helping meet your financial goals. Do not think once you have completed your plan A for retirement that you are done. You will need to continue to monitor the progress of your plan toward meeting your goals and be prepared to move to plan B if things have changed. Flexibility and adaptability are key components of any successful plan.

The current statistics on longevity are very telling. As a nation, we are living longer with less money put away for retirement. While this may not be a disaster, it will certainly have an impact on your standard of living in retirement.

I have found one of the best additional sources of retirement advice comes from those who have recently retired. They walk the walk and talk the talk of retirement. I am part of this legion of recent retirees. You can learn from me and from others what it *really* means to retire. Avoid the mistakes we may have made, and take advantage of some of our good decisions to formulate your personal plan. Nothing beats experience.

Another good source of retirement advice comes from a book by Charles Ellis, Alicia Munnell, and Andrew Eschtruth titled *Falling Short*. They spend considerable time focused on your need for and the importance of self-reliance in planning retirement. Discussions include the importance of having both a 401(k) and individual retirement accounts. They conclude ultimately with the three keys to retirement success being based on the following:

- Save more money than you currently are to add additional funding to your retirement accounts.
- Plan on working longer than your full retirement age.
- Delay taking Social Security as long as possible (the current limit is seventy years of age) to increase your monthly benefits for life.

Sound familiar? These are all incorporated in the strategies I have outlined in this book. Financial sustainability in retirement starts with maintaining a low-cost overhead (low investment fees). The real retirement gains come from spending less than you make. This is true throughout your life, not just in retirement.

I have often been asked, "Don't you have to make a lot of money to have a secure retirement?" The answer is no. You do not need to make a lot of money to retire comfortably. I want you to think about money in a totally different way. I have found this concept to be helpful to many people with insufficient retirement funding at age fifty-five. *It is not about how much you earn; rather, it is all about how much you keep.* This concept changes your focus from earning and spending to saving. This is where it must start. Chapter 4 on the role of budgeting outlines how to save and invest more from the same income. Increasing the amount of money you keep for building retirement accounts is the only way I know to achieve a comfortable retirement—that is, unless you plan on winning the lottery! Changing habits is never easy, but it is required if you are going to catch up on funding your retirement.

Newton's third law of finance says that for every action, there is an equal and opposite reaction. In reality, this is referred to as one of the laws of motion, but it has particular application to the financial decision-making each of us face in our daily lives. Think of your paycheck as an example of a zero-sum game. You receive your net pay to spend and/or invest. When you decide to buy any consumable product, like Starbucks coffee or a doughnut, the cost of that purchase reduces the amount of money left to save and invest for retirement. Why sacrifice the long-term investment opportunity that will provide funding for years in retirement for a short-term benefit like coffee and a doughnut? If you can exercise some financial discipline, you will either forgo the Starbucks and doughnut or find a cheaper alternative, like a McDonald's coffee, so you still have some funds to invest. These choices and decisions present themselves daily throughout our lives. I hope you make smart decisions to stay focused on adding to your retirement accounts.

Benjamin Franklin was quoted as saying, "Energy and persistence conquer all things." If you are persistent and apply your personal energy toward reaching a specific retirement goal, you can be successful.

My best advice includes keeping it simple and returning to the basics of financial management. Plan on replacing up to 100 percent of your preretirement income. The conventional wisdom says if you can replace 75 to 85 percent of preretirement income, you should be okay. Why settle for okay? By trying to replace the higher 100 percent of income, if you miss this target by a few percentage points, you will still have replaced more income than the standard formula.

"Go where the money is" was the reported response from Bonnie and Clyde when they were asked why they robbed banks. Another way to reduce expenses is to go where the money is in your personal financial statement. The really big bucks are in your home. Your home equity may be the largest asset on your balance sheet. By downsizing to a smaller house or apartment, the savings in taxes, insurance, utilities, furniture, and general maintenance expenses can be a large number. Reduced housing costs is where to start. In fact, if the savings number is large enough, this may be the only significant expense adjustment you need to make to fully fund your retirement accounts.

What about the potential of lower future returns from the stock and bond markets? First of all, no one knows what future returns will be. No one can accurately predict these markets because they respond to so many different variables. As the saying goes, "Past performance is no guarantee of future results." So in the interest of being a conservative adviser, what actions do I recommend to protect your nest egg from either historically higher or lower returns in the next twelve years? Higher returns are not the issue. If that were to occur, being fully invested in the market will result in you earning more money faster than your original plan. That can be a good thing! Remember—"A rising tide lifts all boats." But if the opposite occurs and we enter a prolonged period of lower-than-historical returns, then you need some protection. The worst thing to do would be to get out of the market and go to all cash. The second-worst action in this scenario would be to reach for higher yields. That only increases risk. Remember the direct relationship between risk and reward? In a lower-return scenario, you need to save more, work longer, and perhaps reduce your expectations for a comfortable retirement. Funny how this recurring theme keeps appearing in this book and from other authors cited throughout this publication. If we were to enter an extended period of lower returns, I suggest you stay fully invested in a diversified pool of stocks and bonds (index funds/ETFs) with very low expense ratios. Lower costs become even more important in a low-return environment.

To develop more comfort with this approach to investing in turbulent times, I suggest you review another book by John Bogle titled *The Little Book of Common Sense Investing*. In this book, he reemphasizes the importance of not trying to outperform the market, avoid market timing, and focus on low-cost index fund investing—sound advice from a recognized market leader.

Save early, save often, and save regularly. This is the key to money accumulation. It really is that simple.

When it is time to begin withdrawing from your retirement account, use the rule of thumb known as the 4 percent rule. It is a general rule that says you can safely take approximately 4 percent or less of your retirement portfolio value in distributions each year and maintain the principal intact. It is a nice rule to remember, and it is easy to calculate. Applying this rule to your retirement number will give you a conservative withdrawal rate. Keeping that portfolio value untouched is a very nice side benefit to use in estate planning. There are more sophisticated models for calculating withdrawal rates, but I like this one for its simplistic approach. Of course, if you need the money for health and welfare reasons, then you may not have a choice on a withdrawal rate. If you choose not to leave any money to family, charity, or others, then increase your withdrawal rate and live it up. I hope you don't outlive your money!

Here is a checklist of my favorite retirement strategies in no particular order:

1. Never incur credit card debt. Always pay off all credit card balances monthly.
2. If you do have credit card debt, put these expenses at the top of your list to be paid first until they are eliminated.
3. Maintain financial self-discipline.
4. Why are you not using the catch-up provisions of additional contributions to a 401(k) and an IRA account for people fifty and older?
5. Understand the basics of how to maximize your Social Security benefits.
6. Invest at least 15 percent of your gross salary in retirement accounts annually.
7. Maximize investments in tax-deferred accounts to add additional compounding to the potential earnings.
8. Be a long-term investor, with a focus on how much money will be available at full retirement age; do not worry about the account balances each month.
9. Be prepared to move your retirement age to seventy from sixty-seven, if you still need more time to reach your retirement-funding goal.
10. Plan on retirement lasting at least thirty years.
11. Transition from a spender to a saver; remember Newton's third law.
12. Have a backup plan to fund retirement accounts if you cannot reach your goal by age sixty-seven.
13. Backup plans should include working longer, working part-time in retirement (semiretired), and reducing living expenses.
14. Delay taking Social Security as long as possible.
15. Ask your employer to set up automatic bank transfers or payroll deductions to fund retirement accounts.

16. If self-employed, set up your own automatic contributions to retirement accounts.
17. Build a cash reserve equal to three to six months of basic living expenses; replenish this account when you draw down any funds.
18. Avoid buying individual stocks or bonds for retirement accounts.
19. Buy stock and bond index funds and ETFs to match the market.
20. Establish an asset allocation and rebalance it, as needed.
21. Maintain investment diversification through index funds containing small-, mid-, and large-cap companies.
22. When purchasing a fixed immediate annuity, remember to include a spouse through joint ownership.
23. Create both a health care and financial power of attorney, in addition to a living will.
24. Review all beneficiary forms for retirement accounts, and keep them current.
25. Assemble all personal financial records in one place to make it easier for your spouse or heirs to manage your estate.
26. For people in good health, working longer is the *best thing they can do* to ensure a secure retirement.
27. Be on the alert for fraudulent scams. Senior citizens are especially vulnerable to bad guys looking for ways to take advantage of older citizens.
28. Keep it simple! A more complicated plan is not necessarily a better plan.
29. Think about money differently; it is not how much you earn, it is about how much you save.
30. Success comes from execution; the best plans are worthless unless you execute on the strategies within that plan.
31. Take ownership of your retirement planning and funding.
32. Consider hiring a professional money manager to assist you in achieving your financial goals.

Make your own checklist, and work every day to stretch your retirement funds. I am not talking about a diet of sardines and crackers or bread and water. All of us have become desensitized to the many ways we spend money on nonessential things. As you approach your retirement years, you already have all the "stuff" you will ever need. What you really need is extra funding to build those retirement account balances. Be smarter about how you spend money.

You may have heard of the seven deadly sins from Christian origin listed below:

- wrath
- greed
- sloth
- pride
- lust
- envy
- gluttony

These nasty human emotions can lead to an immoral life and a path to the dark side, after death. The investment world has its own set of deadly sins. To be a better investor, learn how to overcome these common transgressions:

- Following the herd—avoid momentum and day trading, as these are forms of gambling; what performed well last year is no guarantee of what will perform well this year. Index funds and ETFs remove you from the herd.
- Griped by fear—the markets are going to be volatile. Daily changes in prices are less relevant than long-term future values. The worst fear is failing to take a risk.
- Head in the sand—always maintain a current sell strategy. If things change, be prepared to move on. This may apply more to owning individual stocks or bonds than index funds and ETFs.

- Forget to rebalance—diversification is a way to manage risk, maintain your asset allocations over time, and make adjustments or rebalance annually.
- Overcomplicate the process—Warren Buffet says, "Never invest in a business you do not understand." Keep it simple and sustainable.
- Overpay in fees—the one thing you can control is the cost of investing. Lower fees mean better results. Using index funds and ETFs means you are following a buy and hold strategy with fewer trading costs.
- Knee-jerk reaction—this is all about staying the course. Make a plan and make it happen. Put investing on autopilot with automatic contributions to retirement accounts. Review your plan semiannually, and stay fully invested.

I have reviewed a number of ways to save and accumulate funds for retirement. There are many reasons to save but one of the purest reasons may be the person who wants to be able to help others in retirement. Helping may consist of donating your time and talents, as well as financial assistance. If you have not saved, you will have neither the time nor money to be in a position to offer assistance to others.

One final thought about protecting your accumulated retirement savings and investments. Too frequently, I read or hear about senior citizen fraud alerts and scams. It appears the bad guys have targeted senior citizens as an easy group to defraud or take monetary advantage of. When you hear about some investment that sounds too good to be true, it probably is just that. Make no decisions quickly about making new investments or giving personal data or account information to strangers. Contact one of your trusted advisers to discuss any potential investment, or request for personal data and share these requests. Seeking another person's advice gives you time to think more clearly about these potential fraud scams. Be careful.

I have expanded the traditional concept of how to build a successful retirement income stream. My parents and the generations before me believed in the traditional sources of retirement income as being a three-legged stool:

- Social Security
- employer pension plans
- self-funded savings and investments

My expanded version of this concept now includes a fourth leg for that retirement income stool:

- Social Security
- employer pension plans
- self-funded savings and investments from IRA and 401(k) accounts
- full- or part-time work after full retirement age

The benefits from full- or part-time work after full retirement age are many. The additional income to meet basic living expenses is an obvious one. The not-so-obvious benefits include a better sense of self-worth, continued social interaction with fellow workers, and the ability to maintain higher brain function by having something to think about other than yourself. I encourage you to seek part-time employment that has a mix of purpose and freedom. If your health allows, consider adding this fourth leg of the income stool to your retirement plans.

Chapter 16

....

How to Enjoy Retirement

Charles de Gaulle did not have a good outlook on the aging process, as he called it "the shipwreck of old age." Retirement is not the end of the road, and it certainly does not have to result in a shipwreck. It is that time of life when you are supposed to enjoy the fruits of your labor from a career spanning four to five decades. Retirement is a time when your focus changes from the accumulation of money to the redistribution of your savings and investments through thoughtful spending. John Lennon said it best: "Life is what happens while you are busy making other plans."

Most of us spend the first one-third of our lives going to school, developing our skills and talents; the next third is all about accumulation of things like money, a house, having a family, and all that goes with it; and the last third is usually when we are in retirement mode and we spend what we have put away enjoying retirement. Financial writers call this final one-third of our life the drawdown period. The goal of this book is to give you the strategies to help you accumulate adequate funds to enjoy the drawdown period of your life.

How do you visualize yourself in retirement? Is it sitting around a nursing home waiting for the next meal, or is it a time for renewal and travel? If you enjoy good health, then use the retirement years as a time to reinvent yourself. Start your own business or partner with a son or daughter in their new venture, paint the watercolors you have been thinking about, become a tour guide at your local museum or just volunteer where you are needed. One of the most rewarding methods of retiring is the so-called "ease into it" approach. Avoid the "cold turkey" retirement whereby you suddenly stop work and stay home with no idea what to do next. Easing into retirement involves a combination of work, fun, and learning. Maybe a part-time job or volunteering on a regular basis is your thing. Travel to visit family or friends or to all the national parks and learn about the natural flora and fauna, as well as the animals that live there. Stay busy doing activities you like to do. This is easing into retirement.

I recommend you begin to think about what you want to do in retirement some three to five years *before* you retire. For most of us, this retirement transition phase will involve thoughtful consideration of these types of future activities:

✓ Work part-time—many retirees will need to work because their retirement accounts are underfunded; being semiretired can give you a sense of contribution and meaning while maintaining social contacts and some time flexibility.

✓ Volunteer—there are so many causes that need the help of senior citizens. This is an area where you really can make a difference. Find a cause you can be passionate about.

✓ Take classes at the local junior college—if you live in a college town, you already know the many benefits available to local residents from the college. Learn for the sake of learning. Enjoy newfound freedom to learn about things outside of your past career field. Have fun interacting with younger students. Audit classes without worrying about final grades.

✓ Spend more time with family and friends—this is one of the most endearing, and it offers benefits to you and your extended family. You have a lot to offer from your experience, and the grandkids have a lot to teach you about social media and new technologies. Make this a win-win. Just spending time together will go a long way toward increasing your satisfaction.

- Embrace being a senior citizen, and write your personal definition of what this means for you.

Here are several helpful resources for finding employment after retirement that I have found to be reliable:

- RetirementJobs.com
- Workforce50.com
- RetiredBrains.com
- Aarp.org (tab for Work and Jobs)
- *Don't Retire, Rewire,* by Jeri Sedlar and Rick Miners

Each of us has a different definition of what a comfortable and secure retirement is all about. Let me share some of my thoughts with you on what retirement has meant for me. These experiences may stimulate your thinking about a different retirement agenda for you. Let's start with a major milestone, your Medicare birthday. When you turn sixty-five, you are fully eligible for Medicare coverage. For most senior citizens, this eligibility for our national health care plan will remove a tremendous concern about providing health care insurance for the rest of your life. Unless you work for a large corporation offering lifetime health care coverage in retirement, this issue has probably been top of mind. Problem solved with coverage under Medicare. Review the options available, and choose a plan that meets your needs and that you can afford.

In all the examples in this book, your assumed age has been fifty-five with a full retirement age of sixty-seven. So even though at age sixty-five you qualify for Medicare, you still have not reached full retirement age. You need to continue to work to full retirement age before you qualify for full Social Security benefits. As discussed in chapter 14, working to full retirement age or beyond is very important in achieving higher funding for retirement.

Is it possible to work too long? This is a question that might be answered differently by each of us. I believe working too long can be problematic. Let me share a hypothetical story. One of my farmer friends, who was of full retirement age, retired from a fulfilling career working the land and soon became bored with the lack of structure in his daily routine. He went back to farming and spent another five years enjoying his daily pursuits of driving a tractor and caring for his cow-calf herd. When he decided to retire the second time, he was no longer in good health. Now his days were very structured, with visits to the doctor's office and time spent in and out of the hospital. What he had missed in those extra five years was lost forever. His grandchildren were now older, and he was now restricted in his ability to travel and participate in other family activities. So unless his goal was to have a future headstone or tombstone that read, "Here lies a hardworking farmer; he gave us five more years," then I think he probably worked too long. Time does matter, and each of us have been allotted only so much of it. There is a time to work, and there is a time to retire. Make your decisions carefully.

Enjoying retirement is not just about having the financial wherewithal; it is also about all of the softer issues involved with living another twenty to thirty years. One of the biggest issues for me in retirement was time: what to do with it, and how to stay active and productive? I struggled with an answer to this the first two times I retired. The third time was the charm because by then I was ready, and I had an answer to the time question that has worked for me. I have developed a new perspective about time. When I was younger, time meant a clock on the wall dictated when to get up, when to go to class, when to sit down for dinner, and when to attend the next meeting or meet some self-imposed deadline. Now in retirement my concept of time is different. No longer does the clock dictate anything other than the time of day. I have time to reflect on memories both past and present, as well as imagine the future. I am free to do what I want, when I want, and with whomever. As someone said, "Every day is a weekend when you are retired!"

I have a friend who has spent years compiling stories and anecdotes about his family and friends. He is writing a book with these memories of his family history for the sole purpose of having a reference about his family's background for his children and future grandchildren. He has traced his family tree and found amazing stories about many of his ancestors. His biggest fear has been this history will be lost with each passing generation. The popularity of social media, with its emphasis on the present, does not bode well for archiving family history. He looks forward to regaling the next generations with these stories. Thank goodness he has made this effort to preserve the past for his family. Why not write the next great history story about your family?

My new perspective regarding time allows me to really enjoy the changing seasons. My wife and I enjoy the variations in the landscape that come with each quarterly change of the calendar. Here are just a few observations regarding each season that I never took time to really appreciate while working.

❖ Fall—splendor of the colors in nature; changing leaves falling to become compost for the flowerbeds; cool dawns and crisp air; football games and tailgate parties; sharing a glass of wine with my sweetie while enjoying a gorgeous sunset; the view from our kitchen window changes daily.

❖ Winter—cold air; snuggled in sweaters and coats; dismal days and fog; gray yet refreshing; cozy fires and hot soups; the smell of bread baking in the kitchen; long, leisurely walks with your spouse; finding a new TV series to enjoy on Netflix and binge watching without feeling guilty; family gatherings for Christmas; reconnecting with friends at holiday parties; Super Bowl party in February; a good book; time to reflect and plan our next great adventure.

❖ Spring—a time of rebirth everywhere you look; plants pushing upward after a sleepy winter; "the best of the best of times"; rain and the thunderstorms that accompany; fresh scent of clean air; lots of flowers and new growth blooming; grass growing; trees budding; the hum of lawnmowers again in the neighborhood.

❖ Summer—bright and sunny days; a cheery time; days full of activities; nights under the stars; sitting around the pool enjoying the never-ending display of high energy from the grandkids;

baseball games and hot dogs (why are hot dogs at a ballpark the best?); day trips and well-planned travels to places both familiar and new; why do the seasons pass so quickly?

One of the best resources I have read on enjoying retirement is *Getting Better All the Time*, written by Liz Carpenter. She was a newspaper reporter and served as the press secretary for Lady Bird Johnson in the White House. Her advice for a full life in retirement can be boiled down to these four phrases:

1. Never quit looking for love.
2. Never wait to be invited to a party (throw your own).
3. Never forget where you came from.
4. Never forget there is a cause that could use your help.

Each day is an opportunity to mold into a day of your liking. If you want activity, then go for a walk, volunteer. or take the grandkids to the amusement park. If you want to catch up on reading, then brew a fresh pot of coffee and settle in your favorite chair with a book you have been waiting to read and enjoy your day. Turn off the cell phone to have uninterrupted silence. These are priceless days.

So many organizations and causes really do need our help. Sure, they all want a financial donation to carry on their mission. I have found giving money to a worthy cause is quick and easy, but it also is quickly forgotten. Both you and the charity forget it. Why else would you receive donation requests from them at least four times a year after your initial contribution? Don't they remember you have already given? For me, a more satisfying way to support a charity of my choosing is to volunteer my time and services, along with a monetary contribution. Providing labor for a good cause offers me long-term intangible rewards beyond dollars and cents and a tax deduction for a donation. This is a much more meaningful experience.

One of the best parts of retirement for me has been having the time to discover the extraordinary among the ordinary. I will let you explore and imagine this possibility for yourself. It is remarkably powerful.

Thank goodness, aging is a slow process. We have years before we reach coveted senior citizen status, with discounts galore from AARP and McDonald's senior coffee. The process of getting older involves a physical/biological transformation, psychological and attitude adjustments, sometimes accompanied by memory lapses and witnessing friends and family members suffer with various maladies. While this could be a dismal time, it does not have to be so depressing. Aging is normal and part of life. There's not much we can do about it other than try to lead a healthy lifestyle, staying active and hoping we have inherited all of those good genes from our parents. George Burns, the actor, comedian, singer, and writer, lived to be one hundred and remained active in showbiz up to the end. He said, "You can't help getting older, but you don't have to get old."

Emotional changes, on the other hand, can sometimes be well within our control, as is our attitude. I saw a poster once that really said it all, "Attitudes are contagious. Are yours worth catching?" You are in full control of your attitude, so make it positive and upbeat, the kind others want to associate with. Don't let someone with a bad attitude drag you down to his or her level. Accentuate all the positive feelings you have for life, and help raise that negative person up a level or two on how he or she feels about life. If you cannot change that person's mood, maybe the best thing you can do is leave and let him or her have time to reflect on his or her attitude in a meditative state.

My wife loves to travel. She is so enthusiastic about planning the next trip while I am still recovering from the last one. If it were up to me, I would probably be content to travel once every three to five years. You know what? I am blessed I have a spouse with such travel insight. The best time to do something is when you can! This is assuming you have the financial ability to do so. We always travel within our means; no first-class airfare or five-star hotels for us. We travel economy along with the real people of the world. We stay in a charming B&B or small, boutique hotel that she finds on the Internet. VRBO is a wonderful tool (Vacation Rental by Owner)! Forget organized tours; we like the freedom to explore and do what we want, not bound by someone else's schedule. This works well for us. Don't wait for perfect weather or the absolute best time, or after the next seasonal change or some other artificial barrier to enjoy travel. None of us know what tomorrow will bring.

Always keep your options open and your self-imposed list of things you cannot do to a minimum. I have another good friend who says age sixty is the new fifty and age seventy is the new sixty. I don't know if he is right, but that is exactly how he and his wife live. He recalls while growing up he thought his parents were so old when they were in their fifties; he thought his grandparents were ancient when they were in their seventies. They tended to sit around visiting, playing cards, and complaining about their numerous aches and pains. They were very inactive. What else would a young person think under those circumstances?

As we age, there is no shortage of others who need help. These opportunities are everywhere with friends, relatives, and complete strangers who can benefit from our assistance. People suffering from illness, disability, depression, or mourning the loss of someone can all use our help. It doesn't matter if it is a ride to the store, carrying groceries into the house and putting them away, raking their leaves, or helping them do some online shopping. Sometimes just a kind word or hug or some form of acknowledgment that this person matters is all that is needed. Serving others in any capacity is the reward of a life lived well. Start with your family members who may need some extra TLC, and branch out from there.

I could go on, but I think you are getting the message. Looking at the world differently through our aging eyes can open whole new chapters in our lives. Give it a try and see if you do not feel more alive, involved, and fulfilled, one day at a time.

Imagine your life twelve years in the future. If you have put these seven powerful strategies into motion, you could be spending your retirement years doing the things you most enjoy. No debt, family provided for, and a working retirement plan that continues to deliver financial results for you that will never let you outlive your money. Now that is "living the dream."

CONCLUSION

Still keeping score? How many people have you met who carry around a long list of perceived slights and abuses against them by their peers, coworkers, neighbors, or other family members? The neighbor who blames you for the dead spots in his yard caused by your alleged over fertilization. The associate at work who thinks you leaped ahead of him or her for a promotion, somehow. The fellow church member who doesn't think you are Christian enough because you are not in church every Sunday. The car pool buddy who believes it is your fault he got a ticket for driving too fast because you are always running late. Carrying these worries around with a feeling of culpability is a heavy burden. Time to give it up! If others have offended you, forgive them. If you have offended someone, apologize. Don't stress over the little things. Free yourself from these self-doubts, and have the self-confidence you can do anything. If you can plan it, you can achieve it. You are the only person in charge of *you*.

Having personally witnessed the unprecedented shift that has moved traditional pension plans out from under the corporate benefits umbrella, I am worried the individuals who are most affected by this change are ill prepared. This includes most of you with a FRA of age sixty-seven. Today most companies offer elective 401(k) plans in place of pensions. Have you ever wondered why a 401(k) is not called a pension? It is because this monumental change in direction and responsibility for retirement planning offers no guarantees. Big brother is out of the picture. This change has created a tremendous burden that is assumed by each individual to provide for his or her own retirement funding. Recent innovations including automatic or mandatory enrollment for all employees in a company-sponsored 401(k), unless you physically opt out, is further anecdotal evidence recognizing this problem. Yet saving enough for retirement still remains a challenge for most people.

I have studied this evolving process and concluded I can offer some assistance to anyone struggling to adapt to this new normal. In addition to speaking to groups and offering one-on-one counseling, I wrote this book to expose a broader audience to the transformational financial strategies needed in building a comfortable retirement.

To paraphrase Robert Ingersoll, "Knowing something doesn't give you command of it. Power resides in use, not in knowledge. It doesn't help to be aware of your situation if you lack the desire to correct it." To help put the tools I have provided in these chapters to work for you, I have organized this book in three parts:

- Part 1—Preparation
- Part 2—Execution
- Part 3—Living the Dream

I have also included four exhibits to be used as worksheets. You may want to copy these exhibits so you can reuse them as needed.

There are at least six significant birthdates that carry a high level of importance for retirement planning. In ascending order:

- Age fifty-nine and a half—this is the earliest date you can withdraw funds without penalty from retirement accounts; I recommend you leave funds invested in tax-deferred accounts as long as possible.
- Age sixty-two—this is the earliest age to begin drawing Social Security benefits, although at a reduced amount; I recommend you wait until your FRA before you even consider drawing Social Security benefits.

- Age sixty-five—this is the age you are eligible for coverage under Medicare; it is important to begin the paperwork within the three months prior to your birth date, called the initial enrollment period.
- Age sixty-six to sixty-seven—this is full retirement age (FRA); if born 1943–1954, sixty-six; if born in 1960 or later, sixty-seven.
- Age seventy—this is the latest you can delay drawing Social Security benefits and still earn 8.0 percent annual increases in benefits. You might as well begin to draw benefits now.
- Age seventy and a half—this is the age when Required Minimum Distributions (RMD) begin for traditional IRAs and 401(k) accounts. RMD does not apply to Roth IRAs.

There are always some skeptics in every group that believe the benefits of retirement are overstated or even a myth. If you love what you do as a day job, your health is good, and you have the stamina to put in a full day's work, maybe continuing to work is the best choice for you. Some people who never want to retire have a deep anxiety about their retirement plans. They know they have not saved enough, or they have no hobbies or interests outside of work and their pleasure in life comes from where they work and what they do. Staying with a full-time job is probably the best decision for them.

For the majority of people I have met, some compromise between full-time employment and full retirement offers a better solution. Expect to work part-time in retirement to stay involved in business activities and maintain social contacts. This state of semiretirement may satisfy all of your needs, while you earn extra money to help offset living expenses.

"Never forget who you are." These are words of advice my grandfather gave me when I was young. I think about them often, and I value my small-town roots. Learning to become a saver rather than a spender will enable you to stretch your retirement dollars further. Passing up the instant gratification that comes from the frequent purchase of new, consumable items can become habit. Instant gratification does not last and most often fades quickly.

Most people I know want to be successful and earn financial security. So why are so many of you still worried about your retirement plans? I believe the answer is naturally imbedded in human nature: it is easier to do nothing than something. Call it *inertia,* one of the most overpowering of all our emotions. People invent reasons not to fully fund their retirement. I ask you to consider: *why not you?* If you believe this book has given you some valuable advice, why not apply this advice to solving your retirement dilemma? Break the restraints of inertia, and take positive action today!

Embrace your past, enjoy the present, and look forward to the future. If you will only look, you will see many new joys await. You may be moving at a slower pace because you are soon to be retired and that is okay.

One of the world's most famous theoretical physicists, Albert Einstein, the father of relativity, and the person who labeled compound interest as the eighth wonder of the world, had a sign hanging on his office wall that read, "Not everything that counts can be counted, and not everything that can be counted counts." While I imagine he intended this saying to apply as a rule of science, it also has application to how we choose to live in retirement.

I know it is not easy to save money for anything. When you save for a retirement goal, it seems the need for those funds is well off in the future. It is therefore easy to skip a monthly contribution for now, thinking you will make it up later. This is nothing more than self-delusion.

You are ultimately going to retire. Accept this fact of life. You do not have a choice on retirement, but you do have a choice most of the time on when to retire. You will retire either by your choice, by age, by forced corporate elimination of your position, or by a change in your health that no longer allows you to work. Why not prepare in advance for this inevitable stage of your life and make it enjoyable?

Monthly contributions toward retirement can be put on autopilot through payroll deductions. You can live on less than you are earning, if you will adjust to this reality now. The sooner you make this choice, the better.

If you have been a consistent saver and not a spender, you may still be short of reaching your financial goal. This can be another reason to increase your monthly contributions by following the strategies outlined in this book. In the final analysis, it is all about financial discipline and self-determination. If you want something enough, you can make it happen. The retirement clock is ticking!

Congratulations! You have finished the book. You can be well along the path to achieving a comfortable retirement. I hope this book has given you the self - confidence to implement the seven powerful strategies of a You-Centered Retirement Model. *Time to Catch Up* is an action verb, requiring you to put into motion these seven strategies that will accelerate the funding needed to provide for a sustainable retirement. Make the best use of your remaining work years before full retirement age by fully utilizing the catch-up provisions for both IRAs and 401(k) accounts. These extra investment dollars will go a long way toward meeting your financial goals. I have given you a valuable set of tips, tools, and strategies to assist you in preparing financially for retirement. Financial self-sufficiency in retirement is an attainable goal. Take ownership of your plan, and make it happen!

A You-Centered Retirement Model

Catch-Up Strategies for Retirement Funding

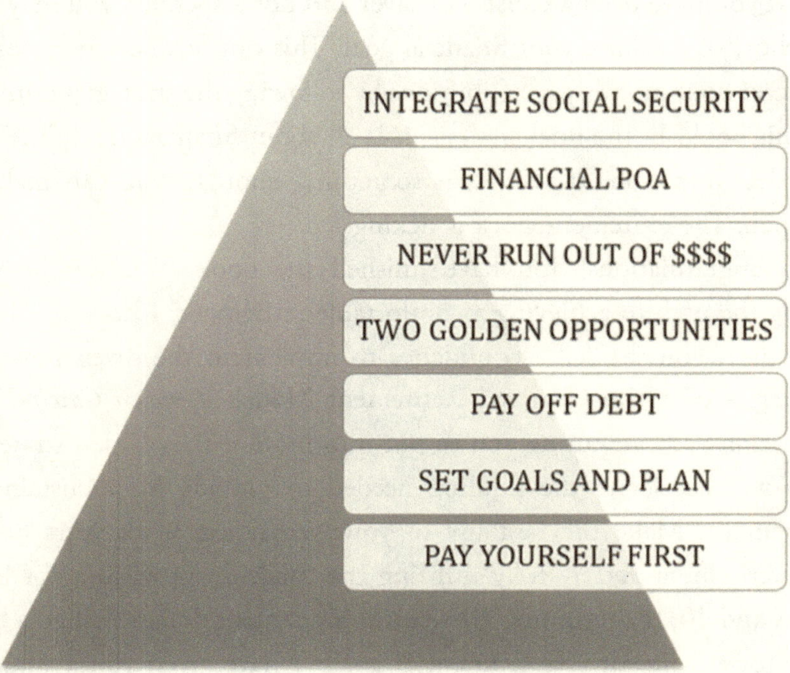

INTEGRATE SOCIAL SECURITY

FINANCIAL POA

NEVER RUN OUT OF $$$$

TWO GOLDEN OPPORTUNITIES

PAY OFF DEBT

SET GOALS AND PLAN

PAY YOURSELF FIRST

Exhibits for *Time to Catch Up*

Exhibit 1: Joint Financial Statement

Exhibit 2: Basic Budget Format

Exhibit 3: Annual Budget Format

Exhibit 4: What Is My Retirement Number?

Exhibit 1

Joint Financial Statement

The following is a general format for a joint financial statement. It is also called a joint balance sheet, as it includes a listing of assets and liabilities for both you and your spouse.

Name _____ Social Security Number_____

Address _____

Telephone Number_____

Occupation_____

Place of Employment and How Many Years _____

STATEMENT OF FINANCIAL CONDITION AS OF _____

ASSETS	DOLLAR AMOUNT
Cash in banks	1. $
Taxable investments (do not include retirement accounts)	
Stocks and mutual funds	
Bonds and bond funds	
Nonmarketable securities	
Restricted or control stock	
Other	
Total	2. $
Real estate owned	
Personal residence	
Vacation home	
Investment property	
Other	
Total	3. $
Partial interest in real estate	
Real estate equities and percentage owned	
Other real estate and percentage owned	
Total	4. $
Loans receivable	
Amount and from whom	5. $

Retirement assets	
401(k) account balance	
Vesting schedule	
Individual retirement accounts (IRA)	
Other	
Total	6. $
Autos and other personal property	
Autos	
Boats and RVs	
Jewelry	
Art	
Other	
Total	7. $
Cash value life insurance	
Owner, insured, face amount	8. $
All other assets	
Total	9. $
TOTAL ASSETS (ADD LINES 1 + 9)	10. $

LIABILITIES	DOLLAR AMOUNT
Notes payable to banks	
Debt payable to brokers	
Debt payable to others—secured	
Debt payable to others—unsecured	
Real estate loans—residence	
Real estate loans—all other	
Life insurance loans	
Unpaid income taxes	
Accounts and bills due	
Unpaid real estate taxes due	
All other debt	

TOTAL LIABILITIES	11. $
NET WORTH (Subtract line 11 from line 10)	12. $
TOTAL LIABILITIES PLUS NET WORTH (Add lines 11 + 12)	

Signature of Person Preparing Financial Statement _____

Social Security Number _____ Date _____

_____

Date of Birth _____

Signature of Spouse _____

Social Security Number _____ Date _____

Date of Birth _____

Exhibit 2

Basic Budget Format

Budgeting is a chore. To make it easier, I recommend starting with a budget for the current month. Using information from this month's budget will help you make a budget for the next month. Keep up this monthly budgeting process for a full year. Then you may feel comfortable making an annual budget based on what you have learned about your total annual expenditures.

Keep in mind the goal of budgeting is to give you the information to change your financial behavior. It is not about tracking every dollar spent!

BUDGET FOR _____(name)_____

MONTH   _____

YEAR _____

MY GOAL FOR THIS BUDGET IS _____

_____

_____

I. INCOME	MONTHLY $ AMOUNT
Salary (net pay)	
Interest, dividends or gifts	
Other income (child support, etc.)	
Total monthly income	A. $
II. Expenses	
Mortgage payment or rent	
Insurance (homeowner's or renter's insurance)	
Utilities	
Property taxes	
Internet, cable, cell phone	
Other household expenses	
Total household expenses	B. $
Food, groceries, paper goods	
Eating out in restaurants	
Other food-related expenses	
Total food expenses	C. $

Health-related expenses	
Medical/dental insurance premiums	
Other health-related expenses like doctor/dentist appointments	
Total health-related expenses	D. $
Transportation bus, train, taxi, car-pooling expenses	
Gas for your car	
Parking and tolls	
Car maintenance	
Car insurance premiums	
Auto loan payment	
Other transportation expenses	
Total transportation expenses	E. $
Childcare	
Child support payments	
Money to support other family members	
Charitable donations	
Clothing and shoes	
Dry cleaning and laundry	
Entertainment like movies, plays, bowling, skating, surfing, etc.	
Beauty care and products	
Other personal expenses	
Total personal expenses	F. $
Interest on bank loans and other debt	
Bank fees	
Prepaid cards, phone cards	
Credit card payments	
Any other fees	
Total finance charges	G. $
Miscellaneous expenses like tuition, school supplies, uniforms, etc.	
Other miscellaneous expenses	

Total miscellaneous expenses	H. $
Total monthly expenses (add lines B through H)	I. $
INCOME (A) MINUS EXPENSES (I) = OVER/UNDER MONTHLY INCOME	J. $

Line J is the amount of over/under income you have to support total expenses. If line I is greater than line A, you are running a monthly deficit and digging yourself into a deep hole. You must reduce some expenses. If line J is not enough to provide funds to meet your retirement account contributions, you must also reduce expenses. Use this budgeting tool to regain your financial balance and begin to make progress toward funding your retirement accounts.

Exhibit 3

Annual Budget Format

This annual budget format allows you to compare month-to-month expenses and quickly identify any trends in expenses. It clearly illustrates how your spending decisions affect how much you have left at the end of each month. You will know what you can change today to save more for tomorrow. Repeat this format for an additional six months.

	January	February	March	April	May	June
Income						
Expense						
Variance +/_						
Housing						
Food						
Transporta-tion						
Health						
Personal						
Finance						
Other						
Total expense						
Over/under income						

Exhibit 4

What Is My Retirement Number?

What is a retirement number? It is how much in savings you need to generate the monthly income you anticipate living on when you retire. This is a very important number, as it will determine your lifestyle choices for the rest of your life after full retirement. There are a number of input factors requiring some research prior to determining your retirement number. Be prepared to research these types of questions:

- What is your estimated longevity? *Use the IRS tables.*
- How much in retirement savings have you currently? *Total of all retirement accounts.*
- What are your projected monthly Social Security benefits? *Use the Social Security website.*
- How much do you think you will need in total monthly income? *Be realistic, and remember expenses may not be reduced in retirement.*
- Estimate both your expected rate of return before retirement and after. *One conservative estimate might be 6 percent before retirement and 4 percent after.*
- What is your estimate of an inflation rate? *Conservative estimates might be 2 to3 percent (the average annual inflation rate the past thirty years has been 3.2 percent).*
- What will be your anticipated retirement age? *I recommend using your full retirement age. For someone currently age fifty-five, the full retirement age is sixty-seven; for anyone born after 1960, full retirement age is still sixty-seven. For birth years 1943–1954, FRA is sixty-six; refer to www.Social Security.gov for full details;*
- What will be your marginal tax rate in retirement? *Depends on your AGI.*
- What will be your annual contribution toward retirement up to the year you retire? *I hope you will contribute the maximum each year to both IRA and 401(k) accounts, including the catch-up provisions.*
- How many years will you be in retirement? *I recommend you plan at least thirty years.*
- Will all of your retirement savings be in tax-deferred accounts? *Yes or no. If no, then how much is not in tax-deferred account and why?*
- What are your estimates of any monthly pension benefits or VA benefits? *Do your own research here.*

- When will required minimum distributions (RMD) begin? *In a traditional IRA the initial RMD must begin at age seventy and a half. Use at least a 4.0 percent RMD as a minimum. If your savings are in a Roth IRA, none of your qualified withdrawals will be subject to income tax;*

Yes, there are a lot of questions before we jump into calculating a single retirement number. Your answers to these questions will have a major impact on the final calculation. Complete the research needed to answer these questions before you go online to use one of the many available calculators. Use this worksheet to assist you in answering the question "What is my retirement number?" Remember the caveat about using online calculators: they are not guaranteed to be applicable or accurate in regard to your individual circumstances. All examples are intended as hypothetical only. They can provide a general number that varies with any change made to the answers to these questions. Your retirement number should be considered a possibility, not a guarantee.

ABOUT THE AUTHOR

Jack Sutherland has been a commercial banker whose career has spanned more than forty years in managing, growing, and developing community banks in multiple markets and states. He started with a BS degree majoring in finance and banking. Later he acquired his MBA, with both degrees from the University of Missouri–Columbia. In between these degrees, he served more than four years of active duty in the US Army, having assignments in Europe, Vietnam, and various locations throughout the United States in the US Army Finance Corps. He was honorably discharged in 1969, having achieved the rank of captain.

He became CEO of a community bank at the age of thirty-five, at the time one of the youngest bank CEOs in the country. He has worked with both large and small banks, finding his most rewarding experience in the community banking space. He has been involved in working with hundreds of small businesses, their owners, and families during his career. He has assisted them in achieving their financial goals. As a result of these experiences, he labels himself a student of business in juxtaposition to a business student. Perpetual learning can be its own reward.

Having experienced the extraordinary shift that moved traditional pension plans from under the umbrella of corporate benefits to the more elective 401(k) and other defined contribution plans, he recognizes the tremendous burden assumed by individuals to provide for their own retirement funding. His experience has shown him the majority of people are *not* ready to assume this responsibility. He has studied this retirement evolution and concluded that he can offer assistance to anyone struggling with retirement planning. He has developed a You-Centered Retirement Model to assist anyone in building a retirement nest egg. He believes comfortable retirement is within reach for all, if they will develop financial discipline, follow his retirement model, and stick with it throughout their working careers. He is a published author, having written *Put Time on Your Side*, a basic approach to retirement planning for millennials (birth years 1980–2000). He continues to be invited to share his insights on this topic by many who are seeking a more comfortable retirement.

Since retiring, he serves on the board of a community bank and another financial services company. He is the founder and managing partner of an alternative investment company specializing in providing financial solutions to small businesses. He has consulted and spoken on topics relating to business, banking, investment, and retirement planning.

He and his wife, Coline, reside in Overland Park, Kansas, where they follow the advice of this book, enjoying their retirement together.

TIME TO CATCH UP

Jack Sutherland

The relationship between time and money

Pay yourself first

Do you know your personal net worth?

The role of budgeting

Goal-setting: develop a plan

What is the best investment plan?

Pay off debt

Two golden opportunities

Which is better: lump sum or monthly payments?

Never run out of money

Alternative use for cash value life insurance

What does it mean to be rich?

Why you need a financial power of attorney

How to integrate social security benefits

A review of my best advice

How to enjoy retirement

www.ingramcontent.com/pod-product-compliance
Lightning Source LLC
Chambersburg PA
CBHW021646120626
46545CB00002B/732